LIFE IN ZION

AN INTIMATE
LOOK AT THE
LATTER-DAY SAINTS
1820–1995

LIFE IN ZION

AN INTIMATE
LOOK AT THE
LATTER-DAY SAINTS
1820–1995

WILLIAM W. SLAUGHTER

DESERET BOOK COMPANY
SALT LAKE CITY, UTAH

Library of Congress Cataloging-in-Publication Data

Slaughter, William W., 1952–
   Life in Zion : an intimate look at the Latter-day Saints,
1820–1995 / William W. Slaughter.
     p.   cm.
   Includes bibliographical references and index.
   ISBN 0-87579-893-4
   1. Mormon Church—History. 2. Mormon Church—Biography.
I. Title.
   BX8611.S55   1995
   289.3'32'09—dc20   95-9140
                                                CIP

Printed in the United States of America

10 9 8 7 6 5 4 3 2 1

To Sheri Eardley Slaughter and her pioneer heritage
and to our children, Danielle and Wes,
who have inherited the pioneer spirit.

I am with you, you men and women of a generation,
  or ever so many generations hence,
Just as you feel when you look on the river and sky,
  so I felt,
Just as any of you is one of a living crowd,
  I was one of a crowd,
Just as you are refresh'd by the gladness of the river and the bright
  flow, I was refresh'd,
Just as you stand and lean on the rail, yet hurry with
  the swift current, I stood yet was hurried,
Just as you look on the numberless masts of ships and the thick-
  stemm'd pipes of steamboats, I look'd.

WALT WHITMAN (1856)

CONTENTS

ACKNOWLEDGMENTS

With this book, as with any endeavor, there are many people who helped and need to be thanked. First, and perhaps foremost, I wish to thank Ronald O. Barney—friend, colleague, and example. Next, I am deeply indebted to my wife, Sheri Eardley Slaughter, for the many ways she showed interest in and assisted with this project. I appreciate all of Jay Burrup's great ideas and help and the use of photographs from his personal collection. W. Randall Dixon was always more than willing to share his vast historical knowledge. I thank my son, Wes, for his computer magic; I don't know or understand what you did, but it worked! I gratefully acknowledge the input of the following colleagues, who are, more importantly, friends: Mel Bashore, Scott Christensen, Robert Davis, Matthew K. Heiss, Mike Landon, Freddy Martinez, Ronald G. Watt, and April Williamsen. A special thank-you to the following photograph archivists for the many ways they facilitated the completion of this project: Susan Whetstone of the Utah State Historical Society; Roy Webb of Special Collections at the University of Utah's Marriott Library; and Drew Ross, formerly of the University of Utah's Special Collections but now a full-time writer and editor of the *Sporting Guide*. Thanks to Kenneth Cannon II. Thanks to Bruce Jensen of St. George for his interest and ideas; Chris Wingo Jensen for his thoughts and insights; David Epperson for the use of his ancestor's quotation; and Jeffery Cottle for his interest, inspiration, and example. I am also grateful to Lyndia Carter for sharing her knowledge of the westward migration (with specific emphasis on the handcart experience). I am grateful to the staff of Panorama Production: Russ Winegar, Mathew Snyder, Bruce Darlington, and Marcie Player. Particular acknowledgment is owed to the following people at Deseret Book: Sheri Dew, vice-president of publishing; Jack Lyon, managing editor; and Michelle Eckersley, assistant art director—they were always supportive, patient, professional, and interested. Finally, I would like to express my appreciation to the administration of the Historical Department of The Church of Jesus Christ of Latter-day Saints. Thank you all so very much!

INTRODUCTION

Get out your magnifying glass. Look carefully and closely at these photographs. Notice the hands, the shoes, the boy in the center thumbing the camera, the book the woman is holding, the hand on the shoulder, the calendar on the wall, the dog under the table, and the body language of the people. Real people. Real places. Images locked in photographs. Lives from the past momentarily captured and retained, enabling us to literally look back at those who came before us. People whose lives were filled with emotion and passion—love, hate, joy, trials, desire, jealousy, trust, spirituality, concern, mirth, pain, luck (both good and bad), foreboding, convictions, affectations, honesty—feeling the same things we feel. Each of these pictures tells a story, and each could command a volume. As we look closely, these photographs come alive for us, and we realize that the events of the past were not some illusory, static historic or administrative "fact" but stories packed with meaning and filled with animated, tangible people.

This volume, unlike other volumes of photographs that have been published, is not intended to document the official history of the Church or various parts of that history. Instead, like your own photo album, it is a fluid glimpse of the past, our past—a look at the people of Zion and the variety of lives that make us a people, all one in the gospel. This cross-section of people, places, and events reflects the continual expansion of The Church of Jesus Christ of Latter-day Saints from an American religious phenomenon to a respected worldwide Church, but it does so in an attempt to portray the individual, everyday lives of its members.

This photograph album is divided into five parts. Part 1 covers the "founding years," beginning with the First Vision and ending with the Saints' abandonment of Nauvoo in 1846.

Part 2 concerns the pioneer years, with Brigham Young at the head of the Church, beginning in 1846 and ending with Brigham Young's death in 1877.

Part 3 begins in 1877 and continues through 1901. During these years the Saints dealt with heavy persecution against polygamy yet were able to complete three temples and achieve statehood for Utah.

Part 4 begins in 1902 with Joseph F. Smith as president of the Church, the first president who was not of the first generation of Saints. This section continues through World War II. This was a period of reconciliation for the Church with the world.

Part 5 begins with the end of World War II and continues to 1995. After World War II the Church's missionary effort rapidly grew worldwide, as did the building of temples.

A Note about Photography

Since 1839, when Frenchman Louis Daguerre invented the first usable photographic process, men and women have been photographically documenting the people, places, and events of their times. These photographers have left us a vital visual record from which we may benefit as with no other historical record.

Daguerre's process was known as the "daguerreotype"; it was a direct positive mirror image produced on a silver or silver-coated copper plate. The next major innovation in photography was the use of collodion ("guncotton") as a medium to hold light-sensitive materials that captured a negative image on a glass plate. The ambrotype and tintype processes, which became popular beginning in the 1850s, were "direct positive" variations of the "wet collodion" process; but like the daguerreotype, the ambrotype and tintype processes could produce only a single image. The pervasive use of photography was realized only after the wet collodion process was used to make negatives, which allowed multiple printing of photographic images on light-sensitive paper.

The procedure to make these images was cumbersome and tedious. Cameras were heavy, and the glass plates were delicate and therefore difficult to transport and store. To properly coat the glass plates prior to exposure, the photographer generally needed a good working knowledge of chemistry. In what was known as the "wet plate process," a solution of collodion and potassium iodide was poured onto a glass plate and distributed evenly over the surface. Then the mixture was immersed in silver nitrate. While still wet, the plate was placed in the camera; then the lens was opened and the plate exposed. The negative was developed within twenty minutes after the exposure. If a photographer was going to take landscapes, cityscapes, or any sort of outdoor photographs, he or she had to bring along the heavy camera, tripod, glass plates, all the necessary chemicals, *and* the darkroom equipment. Often these were transported in a specially designed wagon that also served as a darkroom.

Knowing how cumbersome this whole process was brings greater appreciation for the difficulty of creating images both inside and outside the studio. However cumbersome, it often created clear, detailed images that even today's technological standards are hard-pressed to match. This "wet plate" process was the principal method of photography from the early 1850s through the late 1870s.

The 1870s saw the introduction of "dry plates" with presensitized emulsions, ready-made in the factory for immediate exposure. This relieved the photographer of the trouble of preparing glass negatives and of other laborious procedures. Also, the "dry plates" needed only a fraction of the exposure time the "wet plates" required. Finally, the exposed negatives of this simplified process could be stored for later development, after the photographer returned to the studio darkroom. At the same time, there were continual advancements in the quality, sensitivity, and varieties of printing papers on which the positive images were produced.

As the technologies improved and mass marketing increased during the last decade of the nineteenth century, the number of amateur photographers grew tremendously. In 1888 George Eastman introduced the first "Kodak" camera with roll film (100 exposures). The whole camera, and later just the exposed film, was sent back to the Eastman-Kodak Company for processing and printing; a fresh roll of film (with the camera, at first) was sent back to the photographer.

Also, as more and more amateurs took up the art of photography, manufacturers continued to introduce a variety of new, easier-to-use cameras, film, and print paper. Today almost everyone is involved in photography in some form, from the "point and shoot" hobbyist to the professional with a host of cameras and an arsenal of accessories. But what we all have in common is a desire to document: to capture our lives, our families and friends, and our communities, whether our next-door neighbor or the surface of the earth from a satellite. That is the joy and the mystery of photography—-to breathe life into and to offer testimony of our memories, preserving our recollections of a transitory past.

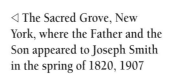

◁ **The Sacred Grove, New York, where the Father and the Son appeared to Joseph Smith in the spring of 1820, 1907**

As a young man of fourteen years, Joseph Smith was genuinely interested in determining which of the many religions was the most correct and which he should join. He recounts his struggle to find the truth: "'If any of you lack wisdom, let him ask of God, that giveth to all men liberally, and upbraideth not; and it shall be given him.' [James 1:5.] Never did any passage of Scripture come with more power to the heart of man than this did at this time to mine. It seemed to enter with great force into every feeling of my heart. I reflected on it again and again, knowing that if any person needed wisdom from God, I did; . . . for the teachers of religion of the different sects understood the same passage of Scripture so differently as to destroy all confidence in settling the question by an appeal to the Bible. . . . I at length came to the determination to 'ask of God.' . . . I retired to the woods to make the attempt. It was on the morning of a beautiful, clear day, early in the spring of eighteen hundred and twenty. . . .

"After I had retired to the place where I had previously designed to go, having looked around me, and finding myself alone, I kneeled down and began to offer up the desires of my heart to God. . . . Thick darkness gathered around me . . . and at the very moment when I was ready to sink into despair . . . I saw a pillar of light exactly over my head, above the brightness of the sun, which descended gradually until it fell upon me.

"It no sooner appeared than I found myself delivered from the enemy which held me bound. When the light rested upon me I saw two personages, whose brightness and glory defy all description, standing above me in the air. One of them spake unto me, calling me by name, and said—pointing to the other—'THIS IS MY BELOVED SON, HEAR HIM.'

"My object in going to inquire of the Lord was to know which of all the sects was right, that I might know which to join. No sooner, therefore, did I get possession of myself, so as to be able to speak, than I asked the personages who stood above me in the light, which of all the sects was right—and which I should join. I was answered that I must join none of them, for they were all wrong, . . . 'they draw near to me with their lips, but their hearts are far from me; they teach for doctrines the commandments of men: having a form of godliness , but they deny the power thereof.' He again forbade me to join with any of them."[1]

▷ **The Hill Cumorah, New York, 1907**

On September 21, 1823, as Joseph Smith prayed, he was visited by the angel Moroni, who spoke of "a book deposited, written upon gold plates, . . . [and] that the fulness of the everlasting Gospel was contained in it, as delivered by the Savior to the ancient inhabitants." On September 22, 1827, Joseph Smith went to the Hill Cumorah and was given the plates from which he translated the Book of Mormon.

Speaking of these events, Oliver Cowdery stated, "A man with whom I have had the most intimate and personal acquaintance . . . actually discovered by the vision of God, the plates from which the book of Mormon, as much as it is disbelieved, was translated! Such is the case, though men rack their very brains to invent falsehoods, and then waft them upon every breeze, to the contrary notwithstanding."²

△ **Emma Hale Smith (1804–1879), wife of Joseph Smith and first president of the Relief Society**

Joseph Smith met Emma Hale while he worked in Harmony, Pennsylvania, for Josiah Stoal. The Prophet wrote: "During the time that I was thus employed, I was put to board with a Mr. Isaac Hale, of that place; it was there I first saw my wife (his daughter), Emma Hale. On the 18th of January, 1827, we were married. . . . Owing to my continuing to assert that I had seen a vision, persecution still followed me, and my wife's father's family were very much opposed to our being married. I was, therefore, under the necessity of taking her elsewhere; so we went and were married at the house of Squire Tarbill, in South Bainbridge, Chenango county, New York. Immediately after my marriage, I left Mr. Stoal's, and went to my father's, and farmed with him that season."

After her husband's martyrdom, Emma Smith married Lewis Bidamon on December 23, 1847. They lived in Nauvoo, where she died April 30, 1879.³

▽ **Oliver Cowdery (1806–1850), scribe to Joseph Smith, one of the Three Witnesses, and associate president of the Church**

While employed as a rural school teacher in Manchester, New York, and boarding in the home of Joseph Smith, Sr., Oliver Cowdery became aware of Joseph Smith and the gold plates. He described meeting the Prophet as follows: "Near the time of the setting of the Sun, Sabbath evening, April 5th, 1829, my natural eyes, for the first time beheld this brother. He then resided in Harmony, Susquehanna county, Penn. On Monday the 6th, I assisted him in arranging some business of a temporal nature, and on Tuesday the 7th, commenced to write the book of Mormon. These were days never to be forgotten—to sit under the sound of a voice dictated by the *inspiration* of heaven, awakened the utmost gratitude of this bosom! Day after day I continued, uninterrupted, to write from his mouth, as he translated . . . the history, or record, called 'The book of Mormon.'"[4]

Cowdery was excommunicated from the Church in 1838. After his excommunication, he practiced law in Ohio and Wisconsin. In 1848, at the urging of his brother-in-law Phineas Young, he traveled to Council Bluffs, Iowa, where he was rebaptized by Orson Hyde. Before moving west, he decided to visit his in-laws, the Whitmers, at Richmond, Missouri, where he died on March 3, 1850.

▷ **The Prophet Joseph Smith (1805–1844)**

"Joseph Smith, the Prophet and Seer of the Lord, has done more, save Jesus only, for the salvation of men in this world, than any other man that ever lived in it. In the short space of twenty years, he has brought forth the Book of Mormon, which he translated by the gift and power of God, and has been the means of publishing it on two continents; has sent the fulness of the everlasting gospel, which it contained, to the four quarters of the earth; has brought forth the revelations and commandments which compose this book of Doctrine and Covenants, and many other wise documents and instructions for the benefit of the children of men; gathered many thousands of the Latter-day Saints, founded a great city, and left a fame and name that cannot be slain. He lived great, and he died great in the eyes of God and his people."[5]

THE HILL CUMORAH

THE THREE WITNESSES

◁ **Oliver Cowdery, David Whitmer, and Martin Harris, the Three Witnesses, who testified to the authenticity of the gold plates upon which the Book of Mormon was recorded**

At first Joseph Smith was told to show the plates to no one, but as the translation progressed, he was informed that special witnesses would be allowed to see the plates so that they could bear testimony of their existence and divinity.

Although each of these men was eventually excommunicated from the Church (Cowdery and Harris returned), none ever disavowed his published testimony. In fact, David Whitmer vehemently stated to the contrary:

"It is recorded in the American Cyclopædia and the Encyclopædia Britannica, that I, David Whitmer, have denied my testimony as one of the three witnesses to the divinity of the Book of Mormon; and that the other two witnesses, Oliver Cowdery and Martin Harris, denied their testimony to that Book. I will say once more to all mankind, that I have never at any time denied that testimony or any part thereof. I also testify to the world, that neither Oliver Cowdery or Martin Harris ever at any time denied their testimony. They both died reaffirming the truth of the divine authenticity of the Book of Mormon. I was present at the death bed of Oliver Cowdery, and his last words were, '*Brother David, be true to your testimony to the Book of Mormon.*'"

Oliver Cowdery died in Richmond, Missouri, on March 3, 1850. Martin Harris died on July 10, 1875, in Clarkston, Utah. David Whitmer died in Richmond, Missouri, on January 25, 1888.[6]

△ **Susquehanna River, Harmony, Pennsylvania, 1907**

On the banks of the Susquehanna River, the Aaronic Priesthood was restored to the earth and the first baptisms of this dispensation were performed. Joseph Smith wrote of this experience: "We on a certain day went into the woods to pray and inquire of the Lord respecting baptism for the remission of sins, that we found mentioned in the translation of the plates. While . . . praying and calling upon the Lord, a messenger from heaven descended in a cloud of light, and having laid his hands upon us, he ordained us, saying: 'Upon you my fellow servants, in the name of the Messiah I confer the Priesthood of Aaron' . . . and gave us directions that I should baptize Oliver Cowdery, and afterwards that he should baptize me. Accordingly we went and were baptized. I baptized him first, and afterwards he baptized me, after which I laid my hands upon his head and ordained him to the Aaronic Priesthood, and afterwards he laid his hands on me and ordained me to the same Priesthood—for so we were commanded. The messenger who visited us on this occasion, and conferred this Priesthood upon us, said that his name was John, the same that is called John the Baptist in the New Testament, and that he acted under the direction of Peter, James, and John who held the keys of the Priesthood of Melchizedek, which Priesthood he said would in due time be conferred on us, and that I should be called the first Elder of the Church, and he (Oliver Cowdery) the second. It was on the 15th day of May, 1829, that we were ordained under the hand of this messenger and baptized."[7]

▽ **The organization of The Church of Jesus Christ of Latter-day Saints; left to right: Joseph Smith, Jr., Samuel H. Smith, Hyrum Smith, David Whitmer, Peter Whitmer, and Oliver Cowdery**

Joseph Smith wrote: "Whilst the Book of Mormon was in the hands of the printer, we still continued to bear testimony and give information, as far as we had opportunity; and also made known to our brethren that we had received a commandment to organize the Church; and accordingly we met together for that purpose at the house of Mr. Peter Whitmer, Sen., . . . on Tuesday, the sixth day of April, A.D., one thousand eight hundred and thirty. Having opened the meeting by solemn prayer to our Heavenly Father, we proceeded, according to previous commandment, to call on our brethren to know whether they accepted us as their teachers in the things of the Kingdom of God, and whether they were satisfied that we should proceed and be organized as a Church according to said commandment which we had received. To these several propositions they consented by a unanimous vote. I then laid my hand upon Oliver Cowdery, and ordained him an Elder of the 'Church of Jesus Christ of Latter-day Saints;' after which, he ordained me also to the office of an Elder of said Church. We then took bread, blessed it, and brake it with them; also wine, blessed it, and drank it with them. We then laid our hands on each individual member of the Church present, that they might receive the gift of the Holy Ghost, and be confirmed members of the Church of Christ. The Holy Ghost was poured out upon us to a very great degree."[8]

△ **Parley P. Pratt (1807–1857), author, apostle, and martyr, ca. 1853**

In August of 1830 during a layover en route to Canaan, New York, Parley P. Pratt learned that "a STRANGE BOOK, a VERY STRANGE BOOK" had just been published in Palmyra, New York.

He later wrote: "For the first time my eyes beheld the 'BOOK OF MORMON'—that book of books. . . . I opened it with eagerness, and read its title page. I then read the testimony of several witnesses in relation to the manner of its being found and translated. After this I commenced its contents by course. I read all day; eating was a burden, I had no desire for food; sleep was a burden when the night came, for I preferred reading to sleep.

"As I read, the spirit of the Lord was upon me, and I knew and comprehended that the book was true, as plainly and manifestly as a man comprehends and knows that he exists."

On September 1, 1830, Parley Pratt was baptized by Oliver Cowdery. One month later, he, with Oliver Cowdery, Peter Whitmer, and Ziba Peterson, was called on a mission to Missouri to preach to the Lamanites.

Parley Pratt was murdered on May 13, 1857, near Van Buren, Arkansas.[9]

▷ **Sidney Rigdon (1793–1876), who experienced revelations with Joseph Smith, was his counselor in the First Presidency and was his spokesman-orator**

While traveling to their mission in Missouri in the fall of 1830, Oliver Cowdery, Peter Whitmer, Ziba Peterson, and Parley P. Pratt visited with Sidney Rigdon in Ohio. Pratt told Rigdon, formerly a Baptist-Campbellite minister, about Joseph Smith, the Book of Mormon, and the restoration of the gospel. Ironically, only one year earlier Rigdon had converted Pratt to the Reformed Baptists. After two weeks, Rigdon announced this new church to be true.

At the Kirtland, Ohio, Methodist church, Sidney Rigdon addressed a group of his neighbors and friends. Parley P. Pratt wrote that Rigdon "addressed them very affectionately for near two hours, during most of which time both himself and nearly all the congregation were melted into tears. He asked forgiveness of everybody. . . .

He forgave all who had persecuted or injured him. . . . And the next morning, himself and wife were baptized by Elder O. Cowdery. I was present— it was a solemn scene. Most of the people were greatly affected. They came out of the water overwhelmed in tears."

Like Parley Pratt, Rigdon almost immediately immersed himself in missionary work. By the end of the year, many of his congregation had joined him in this new religion. He was instrumental in convincing Joseph Smith to gather the Saints to Kirtland, Ohio.

Rigdon was excommunicated September 8, 1844. He died July 14, 1876, at Friendship, New York.[10]

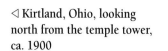

◁ **Kirtland, Ohio, looking north from the temple tower, ca. 1900**

Kirtland, Ohio, was established as a township in 1818, and Church members began gathering there as early as 1831. The town became the first in a succession of gathering places for the Saints. Nearly half of Joseph Smith's revelations in the Doctrines and Covenants were received in Kirtland or the surrounding area.

It is also here that the Prophet organized the First Presidency, worked on his inspired revision of the Bible, created the first high council, directed the move of Zion's Camp to Missouri, established the School of the Prophets, and conducted the building of the Kirtland Temple.

A local history written in 1878 recalled the arrival of the Latter-day Saints in these terms: "Mormons . . . began to come on, and continued to do so, until one almost wondered if the whole world were centering at Kirtland. They came, men, women, and children, in every conceivable manner, some with horses, oxen, and vehicles rough and rude, while others had walked all or part of the distance. The future 'City of the Saints' appeared like one besieged. Every available house, shop, hut, or barn was filled to its utmost capacity. Even boxes were roughly extemporized and used for shelter until something more permanent could be secured."

But as the number of Saints grew in and around Kirtland, so did misfortunes that were brought about by the growing onslaught of anti-Mormon oppression and internal strife. These problems teamed until, in 1838, they finally forced the last of the Saints out of Kirtland and into Missouri.[11]

▷ **John Johnson farm, Hiram, Ohio, ca. 1900; Joseph and Emma Smith lived here in 1831 and 1832**

The Church was headquartered in Hiram, Ohio, from September 1831 to April 1832. In 1831, John Johnson and his wife were converted to the Church after traveling the twenty-five miles to Kirtland to meet Joseph Smith. During this visit, the Prophet miraculously healed Mrs. Johnson's rheumatic arm.

While living at the Johnson farm, Joseph was blessed with many important revelations. Among these was the vision he and Sidney Rigdon received of the three degrees of glory as described in section 76 of the Doctrine and Covenants.

Hiram was also a place of tragedy as non-Mormons grew hostile toward the young prophet and his ever-increasing followers who were beginning to move into the Kirtland-Hiram area. On the night of March 24, 1832, Joseph and Emma were caring for their adopted twins, who suffered with measles.

Joseph wrote: "The mob burst open the door and surrounded the bed. . . . I made a desperate struggle. . . . They then seized me by my throat and held on till I lost my breath. After I came to, as they passed along with me, about thirty rods from the house, I saw Elder Rigdon stretched out on the ground, whither they had dragged him by his heels. I supposed he was dead. . . . They had concluded not to kill me, but to beat and scratch me well, tear off my shirt and drawers, and leave me naked. . . . They ran back and fetched the bucket of tar, . . . and one man fell on me and scratched my body with his nails like a mad cat, and then muttered out: 'G____d____ ye, *that's the way the Holy Ghost falls on folks!*' They then left me, and I attempted to rise, but fell again; I pulled the tar away from my lips, so that I could breathe more freely. . . . My friends spent the night in scraping and removing the tar, and washing and cleansing my body; so that by morning I was ready to be clothed again. This being the Sabbath morning, the people assembled for meeting at the usual hour of worship. . . . With my flesh all scarified and defaced, I preached to the congregation as usual, and in the afternoon of the same day baptized three individuals." Rigdon was delirious for several days after the assault. One of the twins died on March 29, 1832, from a cold contracted during the mob action.

Shortly after this devastating episode, Joseph left Hiram to visit the members in Missouri while his family, along with Rigdon and his family, returned to the Kirtland area.[12]

▽ **Kirtland Temple, 1907**

A committee consisting of Joseph Smith, Sidney Rigdon, and Frederick G. Williams was appointed to oversee the construction of the Kirtland Temple, which began in June 1833. The Saints worked industriously, contributing a minimum of one day a week to the building of their temple.

The sacrifice of the Saints was noted in President Smith's dedicatory prayer: "Thou knowest that we have done this work through great tribulation; and out of our poverty we have given of our substance to build a house to thy name, that the Son of Man might have a place to manifest himself to his people."

Nancy Tracy noted of the March 27, 1836, dedication: "Dedicatory ceremonies lasted two days and they were happy days, for the spirit of God rested on the house and on the people. . . . I felt that I would like always to enjoy the sweet communion with the Holy Spirit as I enjoyed it in that house. Solemn assemblies were called and the elders went from house to house blessing the Saints and administering to and passing the sacrament. Those were truly days of rejoicing for the Saints of God and gave us the strength that was needed for what we afterward had to contend with."[14]

△ **Heber C. Kimball (1810–1868), missionary, apostle, pioneer, and counselor in Brigham Young's First Presidency; ca. 1853**

Heber C. Kimball was baptized in 1832 with his wife, Vilate, and his devotion to Mormonism never wavered. In an 1840 letter to Vilate, he stated: "I have no desire for anything else but to press forward for the celestial world. . . . I know no other way than to be subject to the powers that be. I pray my Father will give me this disposition, for I wish to be in the hand of God as the clay in the hands of the potter. The Lord has His own way of doing His own work, and we have got to submit to Him instead of His submitting to us."[13]

Brigham Young: The Lion of the Lord.

Heber C. Kimball: The Herald of Grace.

Parley P. Pratt: The Archer of Paradise.

Orson Hyde: The Olive Branch of Israel.

Willard Richards: The Keeper of the Rolls.

John Taylor: The Champion of Right.

William Smith: The Patriarchal, Jacob's Staff.

Wilford Woodruff: The Banner of the Gospel.

George A. Smith: The Entablature of Truth.

Orson Pratt: The Gauge of Philosophy.

John E. Page: The Sundial.

Lyman Wight: The Wild Ram of the Mountains.[16]

Among his fifteen compositions in today's hymnal are "The Spirit of God" and "Praise to the Man."

△ Joseph and Hyrum Smith (1800–1844)

Hyrum Smith was a devoted friend and counselor to his brother Joseph. He was also Church patriarch and associate president. Speaking of Hyrum, Joseph declared: "I could pray in my heart that all my brethren were like unto my beloved brother Hyrum, for truly he possesses the mildness of a Lamb, and the integrity of a Job; and in short the meek and quiet spirit, of Jesus Christ; and I love him with that love, that is stronger than death, for I never had occasion to rebuke him, nor he me."[15]

▷ William Wines Phelps (1792–1872)

Before his baptism on June 16, 1831, William W. Phelps was a prominent New York editor of several newspapers. Joseph Smith immediately called upon Phelps's talents by making him the editor of *The Evening and the Morning Star.* In 1845 Phelps gave each member of the Council of the Twelve a special designation:

△ **Edward Partridge (1793–1840), first bishop of the Church**

After initially rejecting the Mormon missionaries, this prosperous hatter and member of Sidney Rigdon's Campbellite congregation was baptized by Joseph Smith on December 11, 1830.

Partridge's commitment to the Church was total; and it was tested, as when in Independence, Missouri, on July 20, 1833, a mob, demanding that Mormons leave Jackson County, dragged him to the public square. He later described the experience: "I was stripped of my hat, coat and vest and daubed with tar from head to foot, and then had a quantity of feathers put upon me. . . . I bore my abuse with so much resignation and meekness, that it appeared to astound the multitude, who permitted me to retire in silence . . . their sympathies having been touched as I thought; and as to myself, I was so filled with the Spirit and love of God, that I had no hatred towards my persecutors or anyone else."

Edward Partridge died in Nauvoo on May 27, 1840.[17]

▽ **Alexander Doniphan (1808–1887), Missouri Militia**

On October 31, 1838, Joseph Smith, Sidney Rigdon, Parley P. Pratt, Lyman Wight, and George W. Robinson were arrested by General Samuel Lucas of the Missouri Militia as they attempted to negotiate a settlement. The next day Hyrum Smith and Amasa Lyman were also arrested and, along with Joseph and the others, sentenced by a secret court to die by firing squad. General Alexander Doniphan was ordered to carry out the sentence. He refused to do so and wrote the following memo to his superiors: "It is cold-blooded murder. I will not obey your order. My brigade shall march for Liberty tomorrow morning, at 8 o'clock; and if you execute these men, I will hold you responsible before an earthly tribunal, so help me God."

Doniphan, who was also a lawyer, would go on to serve in the Missouri state legislature, serve with distinction in the Mexican War, serve as a delegate in 1861 to Washington, D.C., help avoid the drift toward civil war, and then serve briefly in the Civil War as a Union major general in the Missouri State Guard.[18]

△ **Lilburn W. Boggs (1796–1860), governor of Missouri**

When he issued the 1838 "Extermination Order," Governor Lilburn Boggs stated, *"The Mormons must be treated as enemies, and must be exterminated or driven from the state,* if necessary, for the public good."

Ironically, on March 11, 1956, Alvah Boggs, a descendant of Governor Lilburn Boggs, publicly bore his testimony: "My brothers and sisters, I indeed feel humble. I am just a recent convert to the Church of Jesus Christ of Latter-day Saints, to be

exact, just one week. . . . My great grandfather should have done everything in his power to protect any group of people or persons who wanted to worship God in any manner that they cared to worship Him. This he certainly denied the Church of Jesus Christ of Latter-day Saints. I feel very remorseful for my parental lineage for that particular thing. . . . I joined the Church because I believe in my heart this is the Church of God."[19]

▷ **Haun's Mill Massacre**

In 1836 as the Mormons moved into central Missouri (Caldwell and Davies counties), tensions with non-Mormons grew. Missouri was ripe with rumors that the Saints planned to plunder and steal the land from the non-Mormon Missourians, and these rumors were taken seriously. In the fall of 1838, open conflicts escalated in numbers and in seriousness. On October 27, 1838, Governor Lilburn W. Boggs issued the nefarious "Extermination Order," which commanded the Mormons to leave the state or be exterminated. Three days later, during a time of truce, a unit of the Missouri militia made a surprise attack on the Saints' settlement at Jacob Haun's mill in Caldwell County. The attack was unprovoked and particularly brutal, as Margaret Foutz relates: "One day Bro. Evans had an interview with a Mr. Comstock, said to be the head of the mob. All things were amicably adjusted. Bro. Evans then went to inform the brethren. . . . Suddenly without any warning whatever, sixty or seventy men with blackened faces came riding their horses at full speed. The brethren ran for protection into an old log blacksmith shop.

Being without arms, the men were helpless when the mob rode up to the shop and without any explanation or apparent cause, began firing round after round through the crack that was made through the logs of the shop. I was at home with my . . . five children, and could hear the firing of guns. In a moment I knew that the mob was upon us. Soon a runner came telling the women and children to hasten into the timber and secret themselves, which we did without taking anything to keep us warm. . . . And as we went we finally numbered fifty or sixty women and children. . . . We remained there until two o'clock the next morning before we heard anything of the results of the firing at the mill. Who can imagine our feeling during this dreadful suspense. And when the news did come, Oh what terrible news— Fathers, husbands, and Sons unhumanly butchered. We now took up the line of march for home. . . .

"As we were returning, I saw a Bro. Myers, who had been shot through the body. In that dreadful state, he crawled on his hands and knees about three miles to his home. . . . I hurried on to find my husband. I found him in an old house covered with rubbish . . . shot through the thigh. . . . I saw thirteen more dead bodies at the shop, and witnessed the beginning of the burial which consisted in

throwing the bodies into an old dry well. So great was the fear of the men that the mob would return that they threw the bodies in head first or feet first as the case might be. When they threw in three, my heart sickened and I could not stand it more. I turned away to keep from fainting. My husband and another brother drew dead bodies on themselves and pretended to be dead and by so doing saved their lives. . . . After the firing was over, two little boys that were in the shop begged for their lives, but 'No,' they said, 'D___ them, they will make Mormons,' and put the muzzle of their guns at their heads and blew out their brains. What a change one short day had brought."

In all, seventeen Saints and one friendly non-Mormon were murdered; thirteen were wounded.[20]

▷ **Liberty Jail**, Missouri, ca. 1878

Liberty Jail was an ironic name for the prison in which Joseph Smith, Hyrum Smith, Sidney Rigdon, Lyman Wight, Alexander McRae, and Caleb Baldwin were incarcerated from December 1, 1838, until April 6, 1839. They were jailed on the charge of treason.

Conditions in the dimly lit dungeon were squalid and cold. For a bed they had no more than a layer of straw over a hard stone floor. Their food was described as "coarse and filthy."

But Joseph Smith's greatest apprehension was for the Saints (as well as his own family) who were being scattered and forced out of Missouri by order of Governor Boggs. In a long letter written during the week of March 20–25, he revealed his anguish: "O God, where art thou? And where is the pavilion that covereth thy hiding place? How long shall thy hand be stayed, and thine eye, yea thy pure eye, behold from the eternal heavens the wrongs of thy people and of thy servants, and thine ear be penetrated with their cries? Yea, O Lord, how long shall they suffer these wrongs and unlawful oppressions?"

Two weeks after the letter was written, Joseph Smith and the others were allowed to "escape" while being transported to another county. (Rigdon was released on bail in February.) In fact, one guard even helped saddle their "escape" horses!

By April 22 Joseph and Hyrum had joined the Saints who had gathered in Illinois under the direction of Brigham Young, Heber C. Kimball, and John Taylor.[21]

▽ Nauvoo, Illinois.
Temple on the hill,
ca. 1846[23]

△ Nauvoo, the City Beautiful

As the Latter-day Saints were driven from Missouri, they looked to Illinois for refuge. During the winter of 1838–1839, the citizens of Quincy, Illinois, compassionately aided the indigent Saints. After the Prophet Joseph Smith arrived at Quincy, he decided upon the village of Commerce, Illinois, as the place for the regathering of the Saints. When Joseph and his family moved to Commerce, he changed the name to Nauvoo, from the Hebrew word for "beautiful."

Speaking of the new gathering place, the Prophet stated: "The place was literally a wilderness. The land was mostly covered with trees and bushes, and much of it was so wet that it was with the utmost difficulty a footman could get through, and totally impossible for teams. Commerce was so unhealthful, very few could live there; but believing that it might become a healthful place by the blessing of heaven to the Saints, and no more eligible place presenting itself, I considered it wisdom to make an attempt to build up a city."

Two and a half years later, the following was noted: "It is one of the few comforts of the saints in this world, to be settled in peace, and witness the [rapid] growth of their infant city, as a place of safety and gathering. . . . For three or four miles upon the river and about the same distance back in the country, Nauvoo presents a city of gardens, ornamented with the dwellings of those who have made a covenant by sacrifice, and are guided by revelation, . . . in the short space of two or three years, raise[d] a town or a city, glowing with all the arts, improvements . . ."[22]

△ **Orson Hyde, apostle and colonizer, ca. 1853**

On October 24, 1841, Elder Orson Hyde climbed the Mount of Olives and dedicated Palestine for the return of the Jews. This was the realization of a prophecy by Joseph Smith and of his own March 1840 vision. Elder Hyde prayed: "O Thou! who art from everlasting to everlasting, eternally and unchangeably the same, even the God who rules in the heavens above, and controls the destinies of men on the earth, wilt Thou condescend, through thine infinite goodness and royal favour, to listen to the prayer of thy servant. . . . Now, O Lord! thy servant has been obedient to the heavenly vision which thou gavest him in his native land; and . . . he has safely arrived in this place to dedicate and consecrate this land unto Thee, for the gathering together of Judah's scattered remnants, according to the predictions of the holy prophets."[24]

▽ **Joseph Smith preaching to the Indians**

As early as 1830, Joseph Smith sent missionaries to various Native American tribes. In July of 1836, the Mormons were denounced, as they would be in Utah, for "declaring, even from the pulpit, that the Indians are a part of God's chosen people, and are destined, by heaven, to inherit this land, in common with themselves."

At 1:00 P.M. on May 23, 1844, Joseph Smith addressed about "40 Indians of the Sacs and Foxes" who had come to Nauvoo to visit with him. He told them, "The Great Spirit has enabled me to find a book (showing them the Book of Mormon), which told me about your fathers, and Great Spirit told me, 'You must send to all the tribes that you can, and tell them to live in peace;' and when any of our people come to see you, I want you to treat them as we treat you."[25]

△ **Nancy Naomi Alexander Tracy (1816–1902)**

Nancy Tracy and her husband, Moses, converted to the Church in 1834. Thereafter her life was devoted to the gospel as she experienced events in Missouri and Nauvoo, during the trek west, and in Utah. She lost two sons in Nauvoo. The death of her husband in 1858 left her a widow with ten children. She remarried and gave birth to an eleventh child. She died in 1902 in Weber County, Utah.[27]

△ **Joseph Smith Store, Nauvoo, ca. 1885**

In addition to being a store after opening for business on January 5, 1842, this building also served as city of Nauvoo and Church administrative offices, and it was used by various Church and civic committees for meetings. On the second floor of the store, on March 17, 1842, Joseph Smith "assisted in the organization" of the women's Relief Society.

Nancy Tracy relates: "The work on the temple had commenced and the basement was nearly completed. Elders were being sent out to the nations to preach the gospel. Emigrants were coming in from different parts of the earth, and the Kingdom was rolling on. At about this time the Relief Society was organized with Emma Smith as President and Eliza R. Snow as secretary. I was a member of this first Society. It was organized for the relief of the poor and every other noble purpose that comes within woman's sphere of action. Many good instructions were given at these meetings. Sometimes Brother Joseph would come and instruct us. At one time in particular I remember of Emma bringing him in and he prayed at the opening of the meeting. He was full of the spirit of God. His whole body shook and his face shone and look[ed] almost transparent."[26]

▷ **Nauvoo Temple,
ca. 1845–1846**

Construction of the Nauvoo Temple was begun in March of 1841 and occupied much of the Saints' emotional, spiritual, and physical energies until they left the city in 1846. As sections of the temple were completed, they were dedicated and used. However, to avoid potential mob action (anti-Mormons were attempting to destroy the temple), a private dedication took place on April 30, 1846, followed by a public dedication on May 1–3, 1846.

Men and women donated to the cause of finishing their House of the Lord. Many were willing to forego the few comforts they had, as Elizabeth Kirby recounts in her reminiscence: "About this time [November 18, 1843], it was taught in our meetings that we would have to sacrifice our idols in order to be saved. I could not think of anything that would grieve me to part with in my possession, except Francis Kirby's [her husband's] watch. So, I gave it to help build the Nauvoo Temple and everything else that I could possibly spare and the last few dollars that I had in the world, which altogether amounted to nearly $50."[28]

△ **The Jail at Carthage, Illinois, ca. 1885**

Joseph and Hyrum Smith were murdered at Carthage Jail on June 27, 1844, by a mob comprised of rogue Illinois state militia members; the Smiths were assumed to be under Governor Thomas Ford's guarantee of safety. John Taylor and Willard Richards were with the Prophet and his brother during the assassination. Richards sent this short note to Nauvoo; it speaks volumes:

"Carthage Jail, 8:05 o'clock, P.M., June 27th, 1844.

"Joseph and Hyrum are dead. Taylor wounded, not very badly. I am well. Our guard was forced, as we believe, by a band of Missourians from 100 to 200. The job was done in an instant, and the party fled towards Nauvoo instantly. This is as I believe it. The citizens here are afraid of the Mormons attacking them. I promise them no! [signed] W. Richards."

The murder of the Prophet created a crisis in the succession to Church leadership, which was resolved in August of 1844 when apostle Brigham Young was chosen to lead the Latter-day Saints. The martyrdom also signaled the last days of Nauvoo for the Mormons. By the fall of 1845, increasing anti-Mormon actions and harassment had forced Brigham Young to decide that Nauvoo would be abandoned the following spring.[29]

△ **Lucy Mack Smith (1776–1855), mother of the Prophet**

After the martyrdom of her two sons, Joseph and Hyrum, Lucy Mack Smith described her reaction to this awful event: "After the corpses were washed and dressed in their burial clothes, we were allowed to see them. I had for a long time braced every nerve, roused every energy of my soul and called upon God to strengthen me, but when I entered the room and saw my murdered sons extended both at once before my eyes and heard the sobs and groans of my family and the cries of 'Father! Husband! Brothers!' from the lips of their wives, children, brothers and sisters, it was too much; I sank back, crying to the Lord in the agony of my soul, 'My God, my God, why hast thou forsaken this family!' A voice replied, 'I have taken them to myself, that they might have rest.' . . . Oh! at that moment how my mind flew through every scene of sorrow and distress which we had passed, together, in which they had shown the innocence and sympathy which filled their guileless hearts. As I looked upon their peaceful, smiling countenances, I seemed almost to hear them say, 'Mother, weep not for us, we have overcome the world by love; we carried to them the gospel, that their souls might be saved; they slew us for our testimony, and thus placed us beyond their power; their ascendancy is for a moment, ours is an eternal triumph.'"[30]

▽ Vilate Kimball (1806–1867)

Vilate Kimball's letter to her husband, Heber C. Kimball (who was in the East), expresses the grief and worry of the Saints over the murder of Joseph and Hyrum Smith: "Never before did I take up my pen to address you under so trying circumstances as we are now placed. . . . God forbid that I should ever witness another like unto it. . . . Yea, every heart is filled with sorrow, and the very streets of Nauvoo seem to mourn. Where it will end the Lord only knows. We are kept awake night after night by the alarm of mobs."[31]

▷ Brigham Young (1801–1877) in Nauvoo, ca. 1845

At the time of the assassinations of Joseph and Hyrum Smith, all of the Quorum of the Twelve Apostles, except John Taylor and Willard Richards, were away on missions. The Saints were now leaderless, and it was not clear who should fill the leadership role.

The apostles returned to Nauvoo as quickly as possible. Brigham Young arrived on August 6 from New England to find that Sidney Rigdon had preceded him and was claiming that he (Rigdon), as counselor to Joseph, should be the Church's next leader.

At 10:00 A.M. on Thursday, August 8, 1844, a meeting was held for the members "to choose a guardian, or President and Trustee."

Rigdon spoke first and then Young, who stated in part: "For the first time in my life, for the first time in your lives, for the first time in the kingdom of God in the 19th century, without a Prophet at our head, do I step forth to act in my calling in connection with the Quorum of the Twelve, as Apostles of Jesus Christ unto this generation—Apostles whom God has called by revelation through the Prophet Joseph, who are ordained and anointed to bear off the keys of the kingdom of God in all the world."

The vote of the members was overwhelmingly in favor of Brigham Young and the Twelve to lead the Church.[32]

◁ **The widowed Emma Smith holding her son David Hyrum, who was born on November 17, 1844, five months after his father's martyrdom**

Eliza R. Snow wrote a poem in honor of the birth of David Hyrum Smith:

Sinless as celestial spirits—
    Lovely as a morning flow'r,
Comes the smiling infant stranger
    In an evil-omen'd hour.

Not to share a father's fondness—
    Not to know its father's worth—
By the arm of persecution
    'Tis an orphan at its birth!

Thou may'st draw from love
    and kindness
    All a mother can bestow;
But alas! on earth, a father
    Thou art destin'd not to know!

David Hyrum Smith grew up in Nauvoo and later joined the Reorganized Church of Jesus Christ of Latter Day Saints, which was led by his brother Joseph Smith III. David spent time in Utah as a missionary for his church. He was an effective speaker and an able artist, and he was known for his sense of humor and intelligence.

Unfortunately, in 1877 he was institutionalized in an asylum in Elgin, Illinois, because of a "developing insanity." He remained there until his death in 1904.[33]

△ **A daguerreotype taken in Nauvoo of Willard Richards, his wife Jennetta, and their son Heber John**

Willard Richards's journal entry for March 26, 1845, states: "10 [A.M.] went to Foster's, daguerreotype with Jennetta and Heber John."

Jennetta Richards, who was born in 1817, married Willard Richards in England on September 24, 1838. She had been baptized a year earlier on July 31, 1837. Two months after this image was made, Jennetta fell ill on the 21st of May. On July 9, 1845, Willard Richards wrote in his journal:

"At day light dressed . . . [Jennetta] very weak. . . . I gave her encouragement as I felt. She said, 'how can I die under such progress?' About sunrise sent for Levi [Richards] [and] about 6 [A.M.] sent for Elder H.C. Kimball, who came and laid on hands and prayed, she revived. Also sent for Father John Smith, John Taylor, George A. Smith. Heber Kimball, John E. Page, Levi Richards, and myself . . . went into her room anointed and prayed for her and felt encouraged. At fifteen minutes past 10 A.M. Jennetta stopped breathing."

The next day (July 10) Richards recorded:

"Sister Durphy, Sessions, Rhonda Ann, Lucy Clayton, and Sister Wilcox dressed Jennetta and put her in her coffin about sunset. Heber [Richards] said 'Pa, will you bury Ma in the garden, if you do I can bear it. If you do not I cannot bear it.' I told him I would bury her in the garden.

On July 11 Richards noted:

"At dinner Rhonda Ann spoke out very pleasantly and said 'Ma is gone away. She is gone to see Uncle Joseph and Hyrum and my little brother.' . . . About sun set laid the coffin . . . in a vault in the S.W. corner of the door yard. . . . [Threw] a dahlia on the head of the coffin in the vault and said, 'I will come and fetch it with her.'"

In 1868 Jennetta's remains were removed from her Nauvoo garden and brought to Salt Lake City for reburial.[34]

▽ **Migration from Nauvoo**

On a cold February 1846 night, a group of Saints crossed the Mississippi River to begin the trek west to the valleys of the Great Basin. After the death of Joseph Smith, the majority of Saints united under the leadership of Brigham Young and made a valiant attempt to continue the building up of the "City of Joseph." But as in the previous gathering places, anti-Mormon sentiment had grown to such unbearable ferocity that President Young had no other option but to move the Saints to the relative safety of the comparatively uninhabited West.

Lorenzo Dow Young succinctly stated the position of the Latter-day Saints: "Now fixing to leave Our Home and al[l] we have except what too wagons can Draw and our Place of Destenation We know not."

A steady stream of Saints exited Nauvoo and surrounding areas throughout the winter and spring of 1846. By the fall of 1846, Nauvoo the Beautiful was virtually desolate.[35]

△ **Ruins of the Nauvoo Temple, ca. 1850**

After the exodus from Nauvoo, Thomas Kane, a non-Mormon friend of the Saints, visited the city (before the temple burned in 1848) and reported: "Everything was [so] still (there) that I heard the flies buzz and the river ripple on the shallow. After a little I thought I heard the sound of human voices—I listened and a minute after heard it repeat so clearly that I knew it to be the distant sound of boisterous laughter. . . . [I] found it made by a large number of drunken men. . . . They had several jugs of strong waters . . . they were drinking heavily; inside . . . the Mormon Temple others, like them were to be found . . . beastly intoxicated, who had much defiled it with their vomit & filth. . . . Things told very plainly the sad story of the Mormons. Here were their homes and their temple trampled [by] those who had driven them forth from them. It was plain how they had been hurried off in haste and without time to make their preparations."[36]

23

▷ **Brigham Young (1801–1877), Lion of the Lord, American Moses, and second president of the Church, ca. 1850**

The April 1852 edition of the *New York Herald* printed a letter from Jedediah Grant (1816–1856), mayor of Salt Lake City, in which he applied an appropriately Western frontier metaphor to characterize Brigham Young: "I can't undertake to explain Brigham Young to your Atlantic citizens, or expect you to put him at his value. Your great men Eastward are to me like your ivory and pearl handled table knives, balance[d] handles, more shiny than the inside of my watch case; but, with only edge enough to slice bread and cheese or help spoon victuals, and all alike by the dozen one with another. Brigham is the article that sells out West with us—between a Roman cutlass and a beef butcher knife, the thing to cut up a deer or cut down an enemy, and that will save your life or carve your dinner every bit as well, though the handpiece is buck horn and the case a hogskin hanging in the breech of your pantaloons. You, that judge men by the handle and the sheath, how can I make you know a good *Blade?*"[1]

△ **Council Bluff's Ferry, Iowa**

Although the initial pioneer migration to the Salt Lake Valley took place in 1846 and 1847, the Mormon wagon trains and handcart companies moved more than seventy thousand Latter-day Saints to the Great Basin between 1847 and 1869.

The latter date was the year the transcontinental railroads were joined at Promontory Point, Utah, thus allowing quicker and easier travel.

As the vanguard Saints of 1847 readied to begin the first massive push toward the valley of the Great Salt Lake, William Clayton recorded the "order for travelling and camping" as laid out by Brigham Young: "[April 18, 1847] At 5:00 in the morning the bugle is to be sounded as a signal for every man to arise and attend prayers before he leaves his wagon. Then cooking, eating, feeding teams &c. till 7 o'clock at which time the Camp is to move at the sound of the bugle. Each teamster to keep beside his team, with their loaded gun in their hands or in their wagon where they can get them in a moment. The extra men, each to walk opposite his wagon with his loaded gun on his shoulder, and no man to be permitted to leave his wagon unless he obtains permission from his officer. In case of an attack from Indians or hostile appearances the wagons to travel in double file. The order of encampment to be in a circle with the mouth of the wagon to the outside, and the horses and stock tied inside the circle. At 8 1/2 P.M. the bugles to be sounded again at which time all to have prayers in their wagons and to retire to rest by 9 o'clock. Tonight I went to bed about 7 1/2 o'clock. . . . [April 19, 1847] At 5 A.M., at the sound of the bugle I arose. . . . At 7 1/4 the wagons began to move." Other companies would have had rules similar to these.[2]

▷ **Chimney Rock, Nebraska**

On Saturday, May 22, 1847, William Clayton wrote in his journal: "Porter Rockwell came in and said he had been on the high bluff about a mile N.W. of us, and had seen the rock called Chimney rock from it, which appeared a long distance off. We have been in hopes to come in sight of it today."[3]

▽ **Hunting Buffalo, Scotts Bluffs, Nebraska**

In her overland diary, twenty-four-year-old Sophia Lois Goodridge, a convert from Massachusetts, noted: "[July 25, 1850] We traveled about eight miles and camped. We passed near a number of herds of buffalo. Our division killed one and brought it into camp. The first division killed two. The feed for cattle scarcer. We saw quite a number of buffalo dead on the ground. We made a rule *not* to kill more than we needed to eat. [July 26] It is very warm today. We traveled about eight miles and camped on the Platte South Fork. Our folks killed a buffalo and brought it into camp. [July 27] Cloudy. Saw two big white wolves. Passed a number of herds of buffalo."[4]

▽ **Mormon camp at border of Wyoming, 1866**[6]

△ **Pioneers on the plains near South Pass, Wyoming, 1866**

Children on the trek westward saw their experiences differently than their adult counterparts saw theirs. Mary Jane Mount Tanner's reminiscence relates her experience in 1847 when she crossed the plains as a ten-year-old: "There were a great many ant hills along the road raised to a considerable height, where we often found beads which were, no doubt, lost by the Indians and collected by those indefatigable little workers along with the gravel of which their mounds were composed. If we were hardy enough to risk a bite now and then, we found much amusement in searching for the beads to string into necklaces. Another favorite pastime consisted of walking far enough ahead of the train to get a little time to play, when we would drive the huge crickets . . . that abounded in some sections of the country, and build corrals of sand or rocks to put them in, calling them our cattle."[5]

▷ **Fording the Platte River, 1866**[7]

△ Fort Bridger, Wyoming, ca. 1856

Established by mountain man James Bridger and his partner Louis Vasques, Fort Bridger was a trading post for Indians, trappers, and emigrants. The Mormons bought out the partnership in 1855 and improved the outpost. Emigrants would rest and resupply here before the last push down Echo Canyon, up and over Big and Little Mountains, down Emigration, and then finally into the Salt Lake Valley.

Forty-one-year-old emigrant Jean Rio Baker expressed her joy at arriving at Fort Bridger: "[September 19, 1851] Arrived at Fort Bridger, and to my great joy, I was able to purchase 40 pounds of very fine fresh beef, I never saw finer in the London Markets, and that is saying a good deal, also as a great favor got 3 pounds of potatoes, for which I paid 50 cents, the beef was only 10 cents the pound."

The outpost was abandoned in 1857, when President Buchanan sent federal troops into Utah to take care of the "Mormon problem."

Fort Bridger remained a U.S. military base until 1890.[8]

◁ Emigrant wagon train, Echo Canyon, 1867[9]

▽ Mormon emigrants near Coalville, Utah, ca. 1867[10]

△ Jean Rio Griffiths Baker (1810–1883)[11]

△ First glimpse of the Salt Lake Valley from Big Mountain

In his journal Apostle Wilford Woodruff recorded his feelings about the first company's arrival in the Salt Lake Valley: "[July 24, 1847] This is an important day in the History of my life and the History of the Church of JESUS CHRIST of Latter Day Saints. On this important day . . . we came in full view of the great valley or Bason [of] the Salt Lake and land of promise held in reserve by the hand of GOD for a resting place for the Saints upon which A portion of the Zion of GOD will be built.

We gazed with wonder and admiration. . . . Our hearts were surely made glad after A Hard Journey from winter Quarters of 1,200 miles."[12]

▽ Robert Pixton (1819–1881), Mormon Battalion member and missionary, ca. 1866

In the winter-spring of 1846, as the Mormons were encamped and readying themselves for the journey West, President James K. Polk authorized the recruitment of 500 Latter-day Saints to go by land to California in support of the U.S. forces engaged in the "Mexican War." The United States had stood by while its Mormon citizens were illegally driven from their homes, and the irony that it was now asking for help was not lost on the leaders and members of the Church. However, Brigham Young spoke at the various Mormon encampments and was able to persuade 500 men to leave their families and enlist in a cause about which many were dubious.

Robert Pixton, an 1842 English convert, enlisted in Company E of the Mormon Battalion on July 16, 1846. The next day he and his comrades began the longest military march in history. He wrote the following, which suggests much about the Battalion experience: "Crossed a 90 mile desert . . . the main body struck some water in puddle holes and camped for the night. Myself and a few of my comrades got in camp at breakfast time next morning, having been left behind from fatigue, and . . . hunger. We had just time to get a bite before the camp broke up, we started out and travelled until late in the afternoon, when we came to a puddle hole with wigglers in it, I was so thirsty that I lay down and sipped a little through my teeth and travelled on and presently came to good water—I thought we should never stop drinking. The mules ran right into it as soon as they saw it."[13]

◁ **Mrs. Young Elizabeth Steele Stapley (1847–1938)**

Born on August 9, 1847, Young Elizabeth Steele was the first child born of the Mormon pioneers in the Great Basin. Her parents were John Steele, a member of the Mormon Battalion, and Catherine Campbell Steele. Young Elizabeth married James Stapley (1838–1920) in 1864. They were the parents of eight children, of whom six grew to adulthood.[14]

△ **First pioneer women of Utah**

These three women were with the first company to enter the Salt Lake Valley in 1847:

Ella Sanders Kimball (1824–1871), wife of Heber C. Kimball.

Harriet Page Wheeler Decker Young (1803–1871), wife of Lorenzo Dow Young.

Clarissa Decker Young, (1828–1889), wife of Brigham Young and daughter of Harriet Page Wheeler Young and Isaac Decker.[15]

▷ **William Carter (1821–1896) plowing at his home in St. George, Utah, 1893**

William Carter was involved in the Saints' first preparations for farming in the Salt Lake Valley. He wrote: "Jul 24, 1847. When we got to the ground chosen by Colonel Markham for our farm operation, Brother Markham said: 'Brother Carter, are you ready to plow?' I answered, 'Yes.' He then said, 'You start from here and I will go to the point I wish you to plow,' which I did and thus plowed half an acre before any other team got upon the ground. [signed] William Carter."[16]

In the photograph: *Next to Carter:* Ellen Benbow Carter.

On the porch, left to right: Isabella Carter and Harriet Utley Carter.

In the middle, left to right: Norton R. Pixton, Frank Bentley, Jr., Willard Pixton, Grace Pixton McEwan, T. Rose Harker, Hazel Isabella Pixton Paxton, Ella Bentley, Harriet Maria Thomas (holding Mary Elizabeth Pixton), and Sarah Carter Harker (holding Joseph C. Harker).

▽ **Great Salt Lake City in 1853**

An 1855 visitor to Salt Lake City wrote this description of the community: "Into this city we made our entry the 25th of September, 1855, at a quarter past three in the afternoon, fifty-eight days after our departure from Sacramento. We entered it by one of the principal streets, and saw to the right and left gardens and orchards, in which the trees, especially the peach, were laden with fruit. . . . A few Utah Indians wandered about the streets, and seemed to us to be very well looked upon by the inhabitants. . . . All the streets are a hundred and thirty feet wide, and run from north to south, and from east to west. They are watered on either side by a stream of clear water, ingeniously brought from the neighbouring mountains. A double line of arborescent willows (*cotton-wood*) adorns each of these streams. The streets cross each other at right-angles, forming squares of houses, or blocks. . . . Each house, at least twenty feet from the street, is surrounded by garden-ground of greater or less extent. . . . The majority of the houses are built of *adobes,* generally in a simple style, frequently elegant and always clean."[18]

△ **Dedication and groundbreaking ceremony of the site for the Salt Lake Temple, February 14, 1853**

Apostle Wilford Woodruff wrote in his diary: "This was an important and interesting day to the saints in the valley & even in all the world. The saints met upon the Temple block in a vast body to break the ground for another Temple. . . . At 11 oclok President Brigham Young Heber C Kimball & Willard Richards got into a Buggy inside the square surrounded by the quorum of the Twelve. President Young arose and addressed the people and said ['] our history is to[o] well known for me to speak of it now. We shall now again attempt to build another Temple. We have tried it many times but have not been able to finish them so as to occupy them for any length of time. . . . Yes it is the will of God we should build a Temple.['] . . . Heber C. Kimball then arose & . . . dedicated the ground unto God & prayed for the blessings of the Lord to attend them in building the Temple & all the public works in Zion. At the close of the prayer the presidency & Twelve walked to the South East Cornor of the ground laid out for the Temple. The ground being frozen President Heber C Kimball comm[ence]d breaking the ground with a pick then President Richards then Orson Hyde Parley Pratt, W Woodruff, J Taylor A. Lyman C. C. Rich E. T. Benson L. Snow E Snow & F. D Richards. Then the ground was broke & President Young took out the first turf. . . . As soon as the turf was taken out . . . people rushed to the hole to get a chance to throw a little dirt out."[17]

▷ **Ara Williams Sabin (1822–1885), his wife Nancy Ann Hanes Sabin (1828–1903), and their firstborn, Ara Williams Sabin (1851–1929)**

Ara Sabin and Nancy Hanes were married in Fremont, Iowa, on May 23, 1850. They were the parents of eight children. After immigrating to Utah in September 1850, the Sabins settled in Grantsville. Unfortunately, they separated in September of 1874. Ara moved to Idaho and remarried; Nancy remained in Grantsville with her children.

Nancy Sabin was an avid gardener and loved writing poetry. Here is an example of her work:

Dost thou remember, love, the Violet
Thou gavest to me, bidding me ne'er
    forget
To think of thee?
Dear Heart! how many a lonely hour
I've gazed upon that lovely faded
    flower
And sighed that memory had not the
    power
To bring thee back to me.

Forget thee? Not a day nor hour
Glides o'er my soul
But brings sweet tender dreams of
    thee,
And thoughts that sweep beyond
    control
Like the restless tides of some deep
    sea—
Tis true, my love, that I remember
    thee.[20]

△ **Handcart Pioneers**

As more and more Europeans responded positively to the missionaries sent to spread the gospel, organizational and financial abilities were stretched in order to bring these new converts to Utah. The handcart idea was begun in 1856 as a way to help the poorer European Saints. The handcart companies continued until 1860. The individual experiences varied, although undoubtedly the worst strain fell upon the last two companies of 1856, the Willie and Martin Companies, who had to be rescued from an early winter on Wyoming's high plateau.

Robert David Roberts's ordeal, however, shows that one need not have been a member of the Willie or Martin Companies to undergo hardships: "Traveling was very hard on us. The hand-carts were hard to pull and the rations scant. . . . The suffering from heat and thirst were terrible and some of the people became so exhausted that they gave up and stopped their journey. . . . I was compelled to walk the last three hundred miles barefoot as my boots had worn completely out. . . . Several of the company died along the way from starvation and exposure. . . . I passed my nineteenth birthday while on the journey, and much was expected of me. I was tired of life. I had never before felt so. Life had always been so full of hope and brightness, but now hope was gone, so severe had been the strain and I felt so near dead." Roberts, a member of the 1856 Edward Bunker Company, was saddled with the responsibility of helping his parents manage his five siblings on the overland journey.

On the other side of the coin, twenty-two-year-old Mary Branigan Crandall (she married Spicer Crandall after her arrival in Utah), who was a member of the 1856 Dan McArthur Company, had no such pressures (she was extensively aided by Dan McArthur) and saw her handcart experience in a different and very rare light: "We did not suffer anything to speak of, only we needed a little more to eat."[22]

△ **Two pioneer sisters, Mary Elizabeth and Emma Chase, ca. 1853**[21]

◁ **Missionaries in Great Britain, 1855**

This photograph is sometimes entitled "The Handcart Missionaries of 1855" because the occasion of the photograph was a meeting to discuss the possibilities of using handcarts to move emigrants from the Missouri River to the Salt Lake Valley.

Top row (left to right): Edmund Ellsworth, Joseph A. Young, William H. Kimball, George D. Grant, James Ferguson, James A. Little, Philemon Merrill.

Middle row: Edmund Bunker, Chauncey Webb, Franklin D. Richards, Daniel Spencer, Dan Jones, Edward Martin.

Bottom row: James Bond, Spicer Crandall, W. Dunbar, James Ross, Daniel McArthur.[23]

▷ **Edward Martin (1818–1882) with his family, ca. 1870**

Martin, who had been in the Mormon Battalion, was the captain of the ill-fated Martin Handcart Company of 1856. He survived to become a photographer in Salt Lake City.[25]

△ **Friends; Brigham Young, Jr. (1836–1903) and James Ferguson (1828–1863), ca. 1857**

James Ferguson was a member of the Mormon Battalion, a lawyer, an actor, and an orator. Brigham Young, Jr., took his place as a member of the Quorum of the Twelve Apostles on October 9, 1868. In October of 1901 he was sustained as president of the Quorum of the Twelve Apostles.[24]

△ **Mary Ann Angell Young (1803–1882), wife of Brigham Young, ca. 1853**

Mary Ann Angell and Brigham Young were married on February 18, 1834, a year and a half after the death of Brigham Young's first wife, Miriam Works. They were the parents of six children, including Apostle Brigham Young, Jr.

Emmeline B. Wells wrote of Mary Ann: "Humble and unassuming in her daily life, true in friendship, and unfaltering to the principles of truth she had espoused and for which she had made such willing sacrifices, thus she continued to be until the end of her earthly pilgrimage. Her life was a labor of love, rich in good deeds that can never die, whose fragrance will be ever fresh in the hearts and memories of those who loved her."[26]

Mark Twain and his brother Orion had the opportunity to visit President Young in 1861. Twain wrote of the occasion: "He [Brigham Young] was very simply dressed and was just taking off a straw hat as we entered. He talked about Utah, and the Indians, and Nevada, and general American matters and questions, with our secretary and certain government officials who came with us. But he never paid any attention to me, notwithstanding I made several attempts to 'draw him out' on federal politics and his high handed attitude toward Congress. . . . But he merely looked around at me, at distant intervals, something as I have seen a benignant old cat look around to see which kitten was meddling with her tail. By and by I subsided into an indignant silence, and so sat until the end, hot and flushed, and execrating him in my heart for an ignorant savage. But he was calm. . . . When the audience was ended and we were retiring from the presence, he put his hand on my head, beamed down on me in an admiring way and said to my brother: 'Ah—your child, I presume? Boy, or girl?'"[27]

▷ **Heber J. Grant (1856–1945),
ca. 1859**

Heber J. Grant was the son of
Jedediah and Rachel Ridgeway
Ivins Grant. He became the
seventh president of the Church.
It was customary in those days
to clothe young children—girls
and boys alike—in dresses.[28]

△ **Social Hall, 1858**

Dedicated in January of 1853, the Social Hall was used for all varieties of social and cultural gatherings.

In a letter dated January 14, 1864, George A. Smith and his wife Bathsheba wrote: "There are two large halls in this city that are almost constantly rented for balls, one called the Social Hall and the other the 13th Ward Assembly rooms. The first rents for $120.00 per night. . . . These parties are got up in a style of magnificence that would seem wonderful in almost any country. Each ball is opened by a prayer and . . . none are admitted but those who are known to be of good moral character, and the parties are conducted by a spirit of order and general good cheer and closed by a prayer or benediction. This is the way our people conduct our balls and all strangers who visit them speak of them in high terms."

The Social Hall was razed in 1922.[30]

▽ **Anne Winward Wood (1834–1866), 1858**

A Christmas bride, Anne wed Samuel Wood on December 26, 1852.[29]

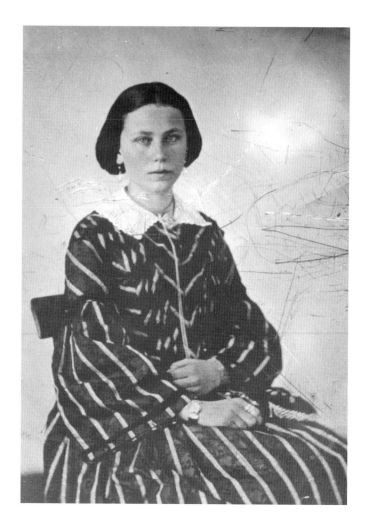

△ **Joseph C. Rich (1841–1908), missionary, age nineteen, 1860**

Joseph C. Rich, a son of Apostle Charles C. Rich, wrote in his journal: "[May 1, 1860] I was called upon by the Presidency of the Church of Jesus Christ of Latter-day Saints on the 6th day of April 1860 in company with about 40 more to take a mission to England to preach the Gospel of Salvation to the inhabitants of that country." Two years later he reported: "Thursday, May 1st, 1862. Two years ago to day since I left my home in Great Salt Lake City. I am through the blessings of God well and on my return after two years experience as a missionary of the Gospel of Peace to mankind, having borne many testimonies to its truths to many hundreds and thousands of God's children in a foreign land."[31]

△ **Ann Eliza Hunter (Rich) (1844–1930), age sixteen, 1860**

Ann Eliza Hunter was the daughter of Presiding Bishop Edward Hunter. On November 1, 1868, Joseph C. Rich wrote to her from Paris, Idaho: "With gladness I improve a few moments to write you, hoping this letter may find you as well as it leaves me. . . . I wondered after I left you if you felt as lonely as I did. . . . I cannot tell when I shall be in the city, it might be in a few days—it might not be for a month, but when I do come I shall expect you to take a trip to the northwest corner of the Temple Block."

Joseph Rich and Ann Eliza Hunter were married on January 14, 1869, in the Endowment House, the location Joseph mentioned in his letter. They became the parents of eight children.[32]

△ **Endowment House, Salt Lake Temple Block**

The Endowment House stood from 1855 until 1889, at which time President Wilford Woodruff ordered it razed. As the name of the building implies, the sacred ordinances of the Church were performed there while the Saints built the temple.[33]

▽ **Ira Eldredge (1810–1866) and his three wives, ca. 1861**

At the time this ambrotype was taken, Ira Eldredge was bishop of the Sugar House Ward.

His wives, left to right:
Nancy Black Eldredge (1812–1895); married July 4, 1833.

Hannah Mariah Savage Eldredge (1832–1905); married February 22, 1852.

Helvig Marie Andersen Eldredge (1844–1939); married November 22, 1861.[34]

△ **Orrin Porter Rockwell (1813–1878)**

British explorer and writer Sir Richard F. Burton met Orrin Porter Rockwell in 1860 and gave the following report of this "Destroying Angel": "Porter Rockwell was a man about fifty, tall and strong, with ample leather leggings overhanging his huge spurs, and the saw-handles of two revolvers peeping from his blouse. His forehead was already a little bald, and he wore his long grizzly locks after the ancient fashion of the U.S. . . . He had the manner of a jovial, reckless, devil-may-care English ruffian. . . . When he heard that I was preparing for California he gave me abundant good advice . . . ; finally, he comforted me with an assurance that either the Indians would not attempt to attack us and our stock—ever a sore temptation to them—or that they would assault us in force and 'wipe us out.'"[35]

brand-new tin cans for their daily allowance of water, uncomfortably suggestive of a tin flavor in the drink. To and fro, up and down, aboard and ashore, swarming here and there and everywhere, my Emigrants. . . . Now, I have seen emigrant ships before . . . and these people are so strikingly different from all other people in like circumstances. . . . The weather-browned captain of the "Amazon" is at my shoulder, and he says, 'What indeed! The most of these came aboard yesterday evening. They came from various parts of England in small parties that had never seen one another before. Yet they had not been a couple of hours on board, when they established their own police, made their own regulations, and set their own watches at all the hatchways. Before nine o'clock, the ship was as orderly and quiet as a man-of-war.'"[36]

△ **The dock at Plymouth, England, 1863**

Unidentified group of people at Plymouth, where the photographer, Charles W. Carter, newly released from military service, was living and learning to be a "photographic artist."

In 1863 author Charles Dickens visited the London docks to report on a company of Mormons who were preparing to depart on the ship *Amazon*. He wrote: "My Emigrant Ship lies broadside on to the wharf. Two great gangways made of spars and planks connect her with the wharf; and up and down these gangways, perpetually crowding to and fro and in and out, like ants, are the Emigrants who are going to sail in my Emigrant Ship. Some with cabbages, some with loaves of bread, some with cheese and butter, some with milk and beer, some with boxes, beds, and bundles, some with babies—nearly all with children—nearly all with

▷ **The Old Tabernacle and bowery, Salt Lake City, 1863**

The "Old" Tabernacle was built in 1852 and was used for various Church meetings. It stood until 1877, when it was torn down to make way for the construction of the Assembly Hall. The bowery was used to hold meetings during the heat of summer; it was removed in 1863 to facilitate the building of the Tabernacle now on Temple Square.[37]

◁ **Lincoln inaugural parade, March 4, 1865; in front of the Lion House and Beehive House**

The *Deseret News* reported that "the 4th of March was appropriately observed by flying national flags upon numerous public and private buildings, a military and civil procession a mile in length, speeches, artillery firing, etc., with fireworks and illuminations in the evening. Considering the snow and inclement weather, the turn-out was very enthusiastic and numerous."[38]

△ **A unique view of Brigham Young showing his back as well as the usual frontal portrait, ca. 1865**

At 11:00 A.M. on August 13, 1860, Sir Richard F. Burton, the famous British explorer and writer, paid a visit to Brigham Young. In his book *The City of the Saints,* he recorded this description of President Young: "I had expected to see a venerable-looking old man. Scarcely a grey thread appears in his hair, which is parted on the side, light coloured, rather thick, and reaches below the ears with a half curl. He formerly wore it long after the Western style, now it is cut level with the ear lobes. The forehead is somewhat narrow, the eyebrows are thin, the eyes between grey and blue, with a calm, composed, and somewhat reserved expression. . . . The nose, which is fine and somewhat sharp pointed, is bent a little to the left. . . . The chin is somewhat peaked, and the face clean shaven, except under the

jaws, where the beard is allowed to grow. . . . The Prophet's dress was neat and plain as a Quaker's, all grey homespun, except the cravat and waistcoat. . . . Altogether the Prophet's appearance was that of a gentleman farmer in New England. . . . His manner is at once affable and impressive, simple and courteous: his want of pretension contrasts favourably with certain pseudo-prophets that I have seen. . . . He shows no signs of dogmatism, bigotry, or fanaticism. . . . His temper is even and placid . . . but he is neither morose nor methodistic, and where occasion requires he can use all the weapons of ridicule to direful effect, and 'speak a bit of his mind' in a style which no one forgets. . . . He assumes no airs of extra sanctimoniousness, and has the plain, simple manners of honesty."[39]

▽ **Brigham Young's daughters, 1865**

This is a portrait of ten of President Young's daughters, who were "well known in the community in the 60's. . . . They were known familiarly in their social circle as 'The Big Ten.' Their attractiveness and lively personality made them the central features in the sets in which they mingled."

Top row left to right: (with married surnames) Zina Card, Eva (Evelyn) Davis, Nettie (Jeanette) Easton, Maime (Mary) Croxall, and Rie (Clarissa Maria) Dougall.

Bottom row: Marinda Conrad, Carlie (Caroline) Cannon, Ellie (Ella) Empey, Emily Clawson, and Fanny Thatcher.[40]

△ **Salt Lake Tabernacle during construction, 1866**

Construction of the Tabernacle began in 1863, and the building was in use by October, 1867.

Visiting from the East in July of 1882, Mary Bradshaw Richards was both critical and complementary when she wrote the following: "Sabbath morning the 30th, we joined the worshippers in the temple [Tabernacle], a building whose egg-shaped roof figures in every picture of Salt Lake City. The Temple [Tabernacle] is a strange and ugly edifice, constructed throughout in defiance of architectural grace, but answering the purpose of its builders. Ten thousand persons can be simultaneously sheltered from sun or rain on comfortable seats; can enjoy perfect ventilation and hear distinctly the voice of a speaker or the faintest note of the organ. . . . We were given seats in the very midst of the Mormon multitude, below the pulpit and near the Lion fountain in the centre of the building. The splashing of four jets of falling water, the chirping of sparrows darting in and out over our heads, and intermittent squeak and babble of at least fifty babies in arms, gave a variety of sound before the singing of hymns began."[41]

△ **William Clayton (1814–1879) and his eighth wife, Maria Louisa Lyman Clayton (1849–1877), 1866**

On April 15, 1846, William Clayton wrote "Come, Come, Ye Saints" in honor of the birth of his and Diantha Farr Clayton's son, William Adriel Benoni Clayton:

*Come, come, ye Saints, no toil nor
    labor fear;*
But with joy wend your way.
*Though hard to you this journey
    may appear,*
Grace shall be as your day.
'Tis better far for us to strive
Our useless cares from us to drive;
*Do this, and joy your hearts will
    swell—*
All is well! All is well!

*Why should we mourn or think our
    lot is hard?*
'Tis not so; all is right.
*Why should we think to earn a
    great reward*
If we now shun the fight?
*Gird up your loins; fresh courage
    take.*
Our God will never us forsake;
*And soon we'll have this tale to
    tell—*
All is well! All is well![42]

▽ **American Fork Brass Band, ca. 1866**

In every Mormon community, there was bound to be a band or a choir of some sort, for the pioneers created and participated in their own entertainment, whether plays, games, singing, or bands.

Kneeling, left to right: Frank Pulley and Martin Hansen.

Middle row: Joseph Robinson, Cyrus Gough, William Grant, Thomas G. Steele, William B. Dunn, and Edward Lee.

Top row: William Paxman, William W. Robinson, Isaac Abel, and Joseph Wild.[43]

▽ **Mormon missionaries in Echo Canyon, Utah, 1867**

The Saints' proselyting efforts continued and grew even as the venture of colonizing the Great Basin proceeded. The missionaries continued to find success in the eastern and southern United States, Great Britain, and Europe, even though anti-Mormonism persisted.

Some members were truly surprised by a call to a mission, as was Eli H. Peirce, who wrote: "On the fifth day of October, 1875, at the Semi-annual Conference . . . I was called to perform a mission to the United States. Just why my name was suggested as a candidate for this mission, and presented at conference for approval or rejection by the people, I cannot say. My mind prior to that time had been entirely given up to temporalities. I had never read to exceed a dozen chapters of the Bible in my life, and little more than that from either the Book of Mormon or Doctrine and Covenants. . . . One of my fellow employees was at the conference; I was not, because I did not care to be. He heard my name called, abruptly left the meeting and ran over to the

telegraph office to call and tell me the startling news. . . . As soon as I had been informed of what had taken place, I threw the novel in the waste basket, the pipe in a corner. . . . Have never read a novel nor smoked a pipe from that hour. . . . Remarkable as it may seem . . .

a thought of disregarding the call, or of refusing to comply with the requirement, never once entered my mind. . . . I was rebaptized, confirmed, set apart, ordained a Seventy and started on my mission, all within a month from the time I was called. Went direct to New York City."

Eli Peirce served three missions in all: "Recapulation: Baptisms, 108; ordinations, 11; children blessed, 37; branches organized, 5; branches re-organized, 1; marriages, 1; meetings held, 249; miles traveled, 9870; total cost, $1320."[44]

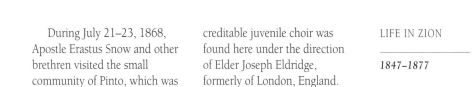

▽ **Pinto Youth Choir, 1868**

Behind the cello is Pinto Youth Choir director Joseph Eldridge. On his right is his daughter Mary Kate. On his left is his daughter Ellen, who is seated next to Ann Jarvis Milne. The others are not identified.

During July 21–23, 1868, Apostle Erastus Snow and other brethren visited the small community of Pinto, which was forty-two miles northeast of St. George. James Bleak, one of the visiting party, wrote: "At this settlement there were nineteen families. It was a thriving place, built in fort style. . . . A very

creditable juvenile choir was found here under the direction of Elder Joseph Eldridge, formerly of London, England. This place was found to have a fair prospect of breadstuffs for a year to come, though there have been serious frosts."[46]

△ **Eliza Roxey Snow (1804–1887), Zion's Poetess and second president of the Relief Society**

In 1867 Brigham Young called Eliza R. Snow to serve as the president of the Relief Society. Over the next twenty years she helped found the *Woman's Exponent* with Louisa Greene, created the Primary Society at the recommendation of Aurelia Rogers, installed the Young Ladies' Retrenchment Association, and was president of the board of directors of the Deseret Hospital Association. As well as being a poet, she was known for her energy and administrative abilities.[45]

◁ Black Hawk War soldiers, "the rough and ready boys," 1866

Bottom row left to right: Henry Snell and Edward D. Woolley, Jr.

Middle row: William Goforth, Solomon F. Kimball, Jasper Conrad.

Top row: Alma Pratt, Conrad Wilkinson, William B. Dougall.

Although Brigham Young's attitude of patience and cooperation toward Native Americans was generally successful with and reciprocated by the local tribes, some skirmishes and battles inevitably took place. In the spring of 1865 a young Ute named Black Hawk led some two hundred warriors in what would become a four-year campaign against the Mormon settlers. The United States federal units refused to intervene, so it was up to the Utah Nauvoo Legion and other volunteers to come to the defense of the settlers of southern Utah. In 1869 a relatively contrite Black Hawk and his forces walked into a Fillmore, Utah, Sunday worship meeting and announced that "their hearts were good and that they desired a lasting peace." The cost to the Mormons: death of seventy men, loss of two thousand head of livestock, and twenty-five settlements abandoned. The cost to the Native Americans: displacement and life on the reservation.[47]

△ **Brigham Young, his counselors, and the Quorum of the Twelve Apostles, 1869**

Photograph taken in the backyard of the Beehive House.

Front row, left to right: George A. Smith, Brigham Young, and Daniel H. Wells.

Back row: Orson Hyde, Orson Pratt, John Taylor, Wilford Woodruff, Ezra T. Benson, Charles C. Rich, Lorenzo Snow, Erastus Snow, Franklin D. Richards, George Q. Cannon, Brigham Young, Jr., and Joseph F. Smith.[48]

△ **Apostle Orson Pratt and others in New York City, 1869**

Left to right: Henry Naisbitt, David Stewart, Warren Dusenberry, Apostle Orson Pratt, William H. Miles, and Joseph A. Young.

Joseph A. Young was in New York conducting railroad business, Orson Pratt was overseeing the publication of the Deseret Alphabet Book of Mormon, and Warren Dusenberry was helping with the logistics of transporting newly arrived European Mormon immigrants to Utah. William Miles was the Eastern States Mission president.[49]

▷ **Indians in front of ZCMI, Main Street, Salt Lake City, 1869**[50]

▷ **Looking east from the top of the Salt Lake Tabernacle, 1869**

Note the temple foundation in the foreground, Main Street, and the tithing yards; and from left to right, Brigham Young's School House, the Lion House and Beehive House, and Fort Douglas in the distance at the foot of the mountains.[51]

△ The Salt Lake Theatre, 1870

Within four years of settling Salt Lake City, the pioneers were producing plays. Brigham Young felt that the theater was a civilizing necessity, and he further encouraged it by building the Salt Lake Theatre, which was dedicated on March 6, 1862. It opened with the play *The Price of the Market*. The rest of the season saw the production of such plays as *Othello*, *William Tell*, *Damon and Pythias*, and *Richard III*.

Between 1870 and the 1920s, the Salt Lake Theatre hosted many of the finest actors and actresses in the United States, including Sarah Bernhardt, John Drew, Edwin Booth, the Barrymores, and Utah's own world-famous Maude Adams.

After sixty-six years of service, the Salt Lake Theatre was razed in 1929 to make way for a gasoline station.[52]

▽ Salt Lake Theatre players, 1870

Standing, left to right: James A. Thompson, Phil Margetts, and Henry Maiben.

Seated: David McKenzie, Annie Adams, Nellie Colebrook, and John S. Lindsay.

In 1912 theatrical manager Michael Leavitt wrote in his memoirs: "In Salt Lake City, one of the largest of the western play-houses, except those of San Francisco, was occupied by a most admirable amateur dramatic company. These supported such dramatic stars as came there occasionally to break the long jump from the East to California. . . . I find peculiar pleasure in referring specifically to one old member of the Salt Lake Theatre Company, born November, 1848, at the foot of the Wasatch Mountains . . . in a log hut in which buffalo hides were the doors and windows. She grew up as a girl in Salt Lake City, and made her debut on the stage of the Salt Lake Theatre on August 25, 1865 . . . in 'The People's Lawyer,' since which time she has been identified and revered by all stage folk. This was Mrs. Asenath Kiskadden, now Mrs. Annie Adams. She has her replica in her daughter, Maude Adams, the idol of the English-speaking stage."[53]

▽ **George Albert Smith (1870–1951), 1874**

George Albert Smith, the eighth president of the Church, was born April 4, 1870, to Sarah Farr and John Henry Smith.

John Henry Smith gave his son this sound advice during his schooling days: "Guard thine honor as thy life, be charitable, virtuous, just, honest and truthful and life's stream will be a continuous scene of happiness and success. Your loving father, John Henry Smith."[56]

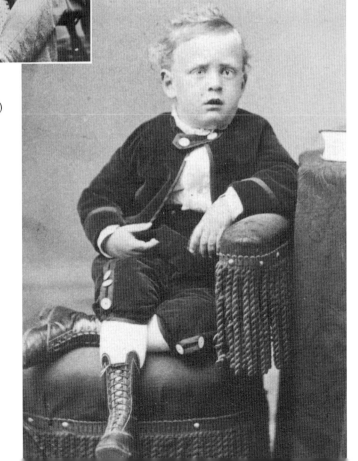

△ **Little Soldier, member of the "Weber Ute" band of the Northwestern Shoshoni**

Little Soldier was born in 1821 at Red Butte Canyon in the foothills of what is now Salt Lake City.

An 1884 newspaper reported the following about his funeral (which was attended in great numbers by both Native Americans and non–Native American Mormons): "In 1874 he was baptized by George W. Hill, in Cub River, Cache County. In 1875 he received his blessings in the House of the Lord [Endowment House], which he appreciated, and to which he always remained true and faithful. . . . He was a peaceful, honest, inoffensive man, a friend to the 'Mormon' people, and was always a welcome guest at the houses of many people in this county [Weber]. Peace to his ashes."

Little Soldier died from wounds he received when stray bullets shot through the wall of his teepee. He did not die immediately but lingered for three weeks.[54]

△ **Newlyweds Sarah Farr Smith (1849–1921) and John Henry Smith (1848–1911), 1866**

John Henry Smith (son of Apostle George A. Smith) and Sarah Farr (daughter of Ogden mayor Lorin Farr) were married on October 20, 1866. Fourteen years later he would be ordained an apostle on October 27, 1880.[55]

△ **President Brigham Young and party at the confluence of the Colorado River and the Virgin River, March 1870**

Seated in the center, left to right: John P. Squires (next to rifles), John W. Young, Brigham Young, Jr., Daniel H. Wells (on the chair), unknown, Brigham Young, and George A. Smith.

Standing behind center row, left to right: (beginning with man in a white coat, just behind John W. Young) Lorenzo Dow Young, unknown, Amelia Folsom Young, John Taylor, unknown, Minerva W. Snow (wife of Erastus Snow), and Bathsheba Smith (wife of George A. Smith).

Charles R. Savage noted in his diary: "Friday, February 25, 1870 the party left Salt Lake City for Dixieland in wagons, carriages or any other vehicle available. . . . [Thursday, March 17] As we travelled on, everything looked very forbidding and unworthy as we approached the Colorado River; it looked still worse at the junction [of] the Virgin and Colorado Rivers. . . . We camped that night on the plateau in full view of the river. [Friday, March 18] This morning after taking pictures of a group of the persons visiting the Colorado, I started with five of Bro. Asay's sons for the Black Canyon of the Colorado."[57]

◁ Samuel D. (1831–1929) and Amanda L. (1844–1925) Chambers, ca. 1908

Samuel Chambers first learned about the Church while he was a thirteen-year-old slave in Mississippi. After the Civil War in 1869, Chambers was able to move to Utah with his wife and son. He was a member of the Salt Lake City 8th Ward. In 1873 he bore his testimony: "I know we are the people of God, we have been led to these peaceful vallies of the mountains, and we enjoy life and many other blessings. I don't get tired of being with the Latter-day Saints, nor of being one of them. . . . I thank God, for my soul burns with love for the many blessings I enjoy. I've been blest from youth up, although in bondage for 20 years after receiving the gospel, yet I kept the faith. I thank God that I ever gathered with the Saints."[58]

▽ **St. George Temple under construction, 1875**

The site for the St. George Temple was selected by Brigham Young in 1871, and he presided over its dedication April 6–8, 1877. It was the first temple completed in Utah.[59]

◁ **Dimick Huntington (1808–1879), Mormon Battalion member, Indian interpreter and missionary, and patriarch**

The year 1875 was the zenith of a "massive movement" of Native Americans seeking to join the Church. Doing so was both a practical and spiritual answer to some very temporal needs as the white population's encroachment led to diminishing options for the Native Americans.

On June 6, 1875, Dimick Huntington wrote to Joseph F. Smith: "Last Thursday night the President talked straight. . . . Said the Lord would take the Lamanites to help carry on the work. They are coming in by hundreds. There has been 2,000 baptized already. I have more or less to baptize every week. I have a baptismal font right before my door, in a house, filled with good pure water, where we administer the ordinance. . . . O Joseph, how I do rejoice in it! They are coming in by hundreds to investigate, are satisfied and are baptized."[60]

▷ **Baptism of Shivwits, 1875**

This photograph of the baptism of members of the Shivwit tribe of southern Utah was taken by Charles R. Savage in March of 1875. Of this event, Savage stated: "As we were leaving St. George for the desert, we saw a great gathering of Indians near a pool north of the city. We found on arriving there that Qui-tuss and 130 of his tribe, composing part of the Shebit nation, were about to be baptized. The men and women were assembled in groups and appeared to feel as though they were about to do some important act. Their manner was as simple and childlike as could be. Bro. A. P. Hardy [standing at right] acted as interpreter, and when he announced that they would engage in prayer, these swarthy and fierce denizens of the mountains knelt before our Eternal Father with more earnestness of manner than some of their white brethren. I shall not forget the sight— some three or four hundred persons kneeling, Indians and Caucasians, side by side; men who had faced one another with deadly rifles, seeking each other's blood, were mingled together to perform an act of eternal brotherhood."

Performing the baptism is Daniel D. McArthur.[61]

▷ **Quarrying granite for the construction of the Salt Lake Temple; Little Cottonwood Canyon, ca. 1875**

William Kuhre remembered his days as a boy working in the quarry for the Salt Lake Temple: "I never worked as a quarryman, being too young for that job. I did serve as a drill packer for a period. It was my duty to carry the sharpened drills from the blacksmith shop to the quarry men at the various places where they were working, and then to gather up the dulled or broken drills and return to the shop for sharpening. . . . There were several nationalities represented among the men. There were Scottish, English, Welsh, Scandinavian countries and Americans. The English sometimes got into an argument with the Welsh, but the Welsh would top it off by saying, 'Wales was Wales before England was born, you see.'"[62]

◁ **Thirteenth Ward Relief Society Sisters, 1875**

Back row, left to right: Emmeline B. Wells (assistant secretary), Elizabeth Goddard (secretary), and Marry Musser.

Front row: Maggie Mitchell, Rachel Ridgeway Grant (president), and Bathsheba Smith (counselor).

Rachel Grant was the president of the Thirteenth Ward Relief Society for thirty-five years; at the same time this widowed mother ran a boarding house.

On July 1, 1875, the Relief Society met, and President Rachel Ridgeway Grant addressed the sisters, stating that she "was pleased with the spirit of the meeting. . . . Felt that many gave who had not much to spare. Referred to the liberality in giving our means for doing good and building up the Kingdom of God. He always blest such and rewarded them accordingly. It was a great privilege to be engaged in the work of the Lord."[63]

▽ **Salt Lake Temple foundation and Tabernacle, ca. 1875**[64]

▷ **Salt Lake Tabernacle adorned for Brigham Young's funeral service, 1877**

Brigham Young died on August 29 and was buried on September 2, 1877. As part of his funeral address, President Young's counselor and close friend, Daniel H. Wells, expressed these sentiments: "I arise with an aching heart, but cannot let pass this opportunity of paying at least a tribute of respect to our departed friend and brother, who has just stepped behind the veil. I can only say, let the silent tears fall that it may give relief to the troubled heart; for we have lost our counselor, our friend, our president. . . . I have no desire or wish to multiply words, feeling that it is rather a time to mourn. Goodbye, Brother Brigham, until the morning of the resurrection day, when thy lifelong companions who will soon follow after will met thee in peace and joy."[65]

▷ Brigham Young, June 1, 1876[66]

△ Brigham Young's grave site,
on 1st Avenue between
State Street and "A" Street,
Salt Lake City, ca. 1885[67]

PART THREE

▷ **Emmeline B. Wells (1828–1921) in Washington, D.C., ca. 1879**

Emmeline Wells, a plural wife of Daniel H. Wells and the mother of five daughters, was a dynamic force in religious, civic, and political concerns. This picture was taken when she attended a National Women's Suffrage Association convention in the U.S. capital. She was the editor of the *Woman's Exponent* from 1877 to 1914. She wrote editorials on such women's issues as voting rights, equal pay, sound exercise, sensible dress, and the recognition of women's intellectual and spiritual gifts. She declared her concern about women not being taken seriously: "See the manner in which ladies—a term for which I have little reverence or respect—are treated in all public places! . . . She must be preserved from the slightest blast of trouble, petted, carressed, dressed to attract attention, taught accomplishments that minister to man's gratification; in other words, she must be treated as a glittering and fragile toy, a thing without brains or soul, placed on a tinselled and unsubstantial pedestal by man, as her worshipper."

In 1910 President Joseph F. Smith set her apart as president of the Relief Society, a position she held until just before her death in 1921.[1]

△ **Heber J. Grant and the Salt Lake Red Stockings, territorial championship team, 1878**

Front row, left to right: William George, Allie Baker, and Joe Barlow.

Middle row: Oliver Best, Heber J. Grant, and Gronway Parry.

Back row: David C. Dunbar, Richard P. Morris, and Alexander Watson.

Heber J. Grant relates the beginnings of his baseball career: "As I was an only child, my mother reared me very carefully. . . . I learned to sweep and to wash and wipe dishes but did little stone throwing. . . . Therefore, when I joined the baseball club the boys of my own age and a little older played in the first nine, those younger than I played in the second, and those still younger, in the third, and I played with them. . . . When I picked up the ball, the boys would generally shout, 'Throw it here, sissy!' So much fun was engendered on my account by my youthful companions that I solemnly vowed that I would play baseball in the nine that would win the championship in the territory of Utah. . . . [I] spent hours and hours throwing the ball at Bishop Edwin D. Woolley's barn, which caused him to refer to me as the laziest boy in the Thirteenth Ward. . . . Subsequently, I joined a better club and eventually played in the nine that won the championship in California, Colorado, and Wyoming, and thus made good my promise to myself and retired from the baseball arena."[2]

▽ **First Presidency, ca. 1880**

George Q. Cannon (1827–1901), President John Taylor (1808–1887), and Joseph F. Smith (1838–1918).[3]

△ Relief Society of Cannonville, Utah, ca. 1880

Front row, left to right:
Unidentified, unidentified, Mary Miranda Davis Losee, Almira Losee Allen, unidentified, unidentified, Lisa Losee, and Lovisa Cox.

Back row: Sister Cokerhanz, Martha Losee, unidentified, Isadora Losee Allen, Mrs. John Hatch, Alvie Tippets, Christine Merrill, Mrs. John Merrill, Miss Mangrum, unidentified, Mary Aliza Losee, Mrs. Allen, unidentified, and Lavern Caffel.[4]

Thomas C. Griggs

"Take a tract?"

◁ "Take a tract?" Elder Thomas C. Griggs (1845–1903), British Mission, 1880

Elder Thomas Griggs met many unusual people during his mission. He noted them in his journal without passing judgment: "[May 24, 1880; Newbury] Bro. Richard Smith, Chieveley—the old lady keeps shop . . . have been married 50 years come Michaelmas; members of the Church over thirty years . . . very old house—low ceiling. Here they have a daughter named Lucy who stays upstairs and will not be seen of men; she is the mother of 2 'love children'—one in the valley, the other at school. Bro. Willey [Griggs' companion] shouts from [the] bottom . . . , 'How are you, Lucy?' The unseen answers, 'Pretty well, Bro. Willey.' He then tells or introduces me to her. Flora comes home from school— very shy. Get out photos. Bro. Willey asks Lucy to let him come up and show them; 'No thanks' in great earnestness from voice above. . . . Father Smith comes home from work hale and cheerful. . . . [We] have a good sing. . . . Old lady thinks I have a good strong voice. . . . The old folks give us their bed, we carefully mount the stairs[,] pass Lucy's room with rag curtain door, to the cock loft bed room. Get in and Bro. Willey chats with Lucy inquiring when she had been out and she replied [she] had been there 5 years, had been up the street twice, had [a] nervous brain, wants to emigrate."

Thomas Griggs' singing was more than a passing interest. The current LDS hymnal contains two of his compositions: "God Is Love" and "Gently Raise the Sacred Strain."[5]

△ **The Salt Lake Temple,** ca. 1883

In the foreground are Charles R. Savage's photograph gallery and the Council House. On the Temple Block are the Assembly Hall, the Tabernacle, and the temple under construction.[6]

▷ **Plain City, Utah, schoolgirls with teachers, ca. 1884**

These school girls are unidentified, but two of the teachers are, on the left, William S. Geddes and, on the right, George H. Carver.[7]

▷ **The Logan Temple, ca. 1883**

The Logan Temple, the second completed in Utah, was dedicated on May 17, 1884, by President John Taylor. Construction of the Logan Temple began in 1877.[9]

▷ **Plain City, Utah, schoolboys with teachers, ca. 1884**

Notice someone peeking around the corner of the building.[8]

△ **Foundry workers, Logan, Utah**

Left to right: John Roberts, Al Jones, John Wilson, John H. Wilson (boy in front), Carl H. Lundberg, Christian Lundberg, Peter Afflect, William Rozy (in background with hat), John Roberts (boy in front), Gustove Thompson, Rozell Hopkins, Charley Sorenson, Mr. Evanson, George Wagner, and John Carlyle.

These men made the oxen for the Logan Temple baptismal font and the iron fence that encircled the baptistry. Otto Lundberg related this account: "Father [Carl Lundberg, a blacksmith by trade] was asked to build the fence around the [font] in the temple. . . . He felt this a great [privilege] and honor. After much consideration and thought a fence was designed. It required a great deal of steady handwork.

Father would heat the iron posts and then have me hold one end of them with a big pair of pliars . . . while he made the right curl on the top of each post. Then a curl had to be welded on each side to complete the design. . . . It took a lot of time and patience. . . . The oxen surrounding the [font] was another thing father helped to complete. His desire was to have them near perfect as possible. The horns were the big problem as the rest were made in a mold. Many horns were made but to have the right set provide[d] quite a decision. . . . We . . . prayed as only Father could to our Heavenly Father for an answer to this problem. As Father arose the look on his face had changed from a worried, sad one to one of brilliance. He knew which was the right set, he immediately walked over and picked them up."[10]

◁ **The Salt Lake Tabernacle Choir, 1884**

The Tabernacle Choir is serenading on New Year's Day at the home of Bishop John Sharp on "E" Street and 1st Avenue in Salt Lake City.

Sitting in front (with full beard) is the conductor, Ebenezer Beasley. The man with the bagpipes is William C. Dunbar.[11]

◁ **Karl G. Maeser (1828–1901) and the Brigham Young Academy faculty, ca. 1885**

Left to right: Willard Done, James E. Talmage, Joseph Nelson, Karl G. Maeser (principal), Jennie Tanner, Benjamin Cluff, Jr., and Joseph B. Keeler.

Karl Maeser, an 1855 convert from Germany, was the "father of Brigham Young University." In April 1876 Brigham Young assigned Maeser to go to Provo, Utah, and organize the Brigham Young Academy. By August 27 he had sixty-seven students attending the opening of BYA.

Of him, teacher Willard Done said: "The strongest impression Dr. Maeser made on me was of unselfish devotion and unwavering faithfulness. By his life and teachings he made this fundamental in the character of his students. If I ever prove recreant to a trust or faithless to a duty, it will be contrary to the most impressive teachings a man was ever permitted to receive."[13]

▷ **John William Frederick Volker (1859–1932) aboard ship with a group of Dutch Saints emigrating to the United States, ca. 1885**

John Volker, sitting at left, served two missions to Holland and translated the Book of Mormon and other Church works into Dutch.[12]

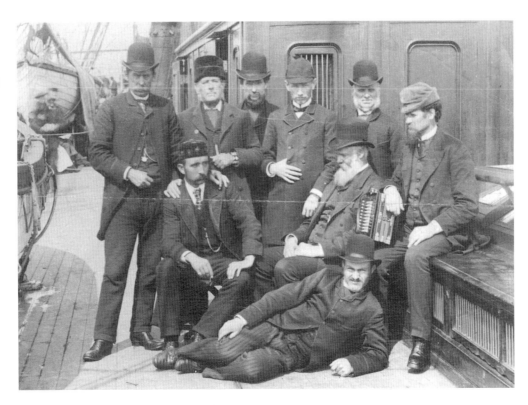

△ **View of casket and decorations in preparation for the funeral of President John Taylor, Salt Lake Tabernacle; July 29, 1887**

President John Taylor presided over troubled times for the Saints. After the passage of the federal Edmunds Anti-Polygamy Act in 1882, persecution of the Saints regenerated. Much of John Taylor's presidency was spent in hiding as a result of threats and harassment from government officials.

Ironically, John Taylor, a British convert, was a great believer in the United States Constitution. At his funeral Apostle Franklin D. Richards stated: "President Taylor entertained the most profound regard for the superiority of the principles of the American government. . . . I recollect well when the news arrived of the passage of those laws which have lately engaged the attention of the people, how with what consideration he sat down and conversed with myself and others upon that subject, and how he carefully and prayerfully adjusted the affairs of his household in a way that . . . no man nor no government could take exceptions to. . . . [He] went into retirement, went where, under certain circumstances he could still serve his brethren, still counsel them in the ways of life, still advise them as a man who was entrusted with the keys of eternal life to the human family, and this he did, blessed be God! until the day of his death. . . . He has died from the legitimate consequences of confinement. . . . When we recount the activity of his life, when we contemplate the dignity of his character . . . and how exceptional it has been, what an example it is for us!"[14]

▷ **Youth of Colonia Juarez, Mexico, ca. 1887**

Front row, left to right: Mary Wright (McClellan), Sylvia Bailey (Bloomfield), Alta McClellan (Whipple), Grace Chestnut, Lila Judd, Minnie Cardon (Taylor), Addie Johnson, and Annie Martineau (Walser).

Back row: Guy Taylor, Joseph Turley, Theodore Martineau, Jess Johnson, Edward Turley, Joel H. Martineau, John Bloomfield, Ernest Turley, and Frank Stowell.

In the spring of 1885 a group of Saints led by Isaac Turley settled in an area of Mexico about 150 miles west of El Paso, Texas. A township was surveyed in 1886, and the site was dedicated in January of 1887 and named Juarez after the famous Mexican leader.

In addition to the ever-present hard work of beginning and maintaining a frontier colony, there was always some time for fun in the form of games, sports, and dances. As one resident wrote: "It was Friday night, the regular dance night. Both hall and the stage had been swept and dusted, and the long benches pushed tight against the wall or shoved into the side rooms. Floors had been candled, the whittler spreading the shavings evenly over the pine boards and carefully tamping each big piece down for a sleek finish. Lamps trimmed with tin reflectors sat on the high wall brackets and swung from the ceiling on strong wires; and light gleaming from them chased shadows from the far corners of both rooms. Dancers arrived in groups, those 'going steady' lingering longest at the doors before separating to join the men and boys along the south wall or the women and girls seated on the north side. . . . It was the social event of the week, and they gave themselves to the mood of enjoyment."[15]

◁ **Dr. Edward Isaacson (1859–unknown), translating the Book of Mormon into Hebrew, 1888**[16]

△ **Manti Temple under construction, 1887**

The site for the Manti Temple was chosen by Brigham Young on June 25, 1875. Wilford Woodruff dedicated the completed structure on May 17, 1888. It was the third completed temple in Utah.[17]

▷ **"Within the Gates":** prisoners for conscience' sake, Utah Penitentiary, ca. 1887

Incarcerated for polygamy, George Kirkham is standing at the extreme right, and kneeling at his right is James Kirkham.

In 1887 harassment and prosecution of Mormon polygamists increased when Congress passed the Edmunds-Tucker Act, which closed loopholes existing in the 1882 Edmunds Act. The Edmunds-Tucker Act also provided for the disenfranchisement of polygamists and the disincorporation of the Church, requiring that its property be escheated to the United States. This Act caused such a financial and legal mess that the Church was not able to pay off all of its indebtedness until 1907.

Living conditions in prison were less than healthy. Rudger Clawson explained that "a man could write his name with the blood of bugs by pressing his finger against them as they crawled along the wall and over the frame work of the bunks. Newly whitewashed walls soon told an awful tale of blood and carnage, and, until the novelty wore off, it was quite amusing to watch the convicts war against their powerful enemies at all hours of the night."

WITHIN THE GATES, UTAH PENITENTIARY.
C.R. SAVAGE Phot.

However, polygamy prisoners made the best of a dreadful situation. John Lee Jones wrote: "Some of the Brethren wished me to join them in making a little music. Some of them had brought their Instruments with them into the Prison. I did not bring my Violin from home. One of the brethren Sent to the city & got a Violin for me to use. . . . So we formed a Band of Musicians (viz) Bro.

William Foster [guitar] of Salt Lake City, Bro. H. Sperry [violin], Bro. Kirkham of Lehi [trombone] . . . F. Tidwell his Banjo, & . . . Bro. Geo. Wood, with his Violin. We would gather . . . in the afternoon in nice Weather in the Prison yard & play marches, Polkas, Quadrills & Waltzes. Somtimes the Prisoners would form a Line & have a grand March to the Sweet Strains of Music from the

band; thus we made our prison life as happy as possible."[18]

On October 6, 1890, President Wilford Woodruff issued the "Manifesto," which officially declared an end to the practice of plural marriage by the Church.[19]

▷ **George Q. Cannon (1827–1901), Utah Penitentiary, September 21, 1888**

Left to right: Unidentified, Charles H. Wilcken, George Q. Cannon, two prison guards, and Franklin S. Richards (Cannon's lawyer).

George Q. Cannon, a member of the First Presidency, had been a missionary to the Sandwich Islands, translated the Book of Mormon into Hawaiian, and been elected a territorial delegate to the U.S. Congress in 1872. He was also a publisher. After being apprehended and then failing to appear for trial in 1886, Cannon remained in hiding until September of 1888, when he turned himself over to the federal authorities. He entered prison on September 17.

George Q. Cannon wrote in his diary on September 21, 1888: "Had another visit from Bro. F. S. Richards and another private conversation with him. . . . Bro. C. H. Wilcken came up also. While they were in the yard a photographer, C. E. Johnson, took two photographs of myself, Bro's. Richards and Wilcken, and two guards, Mr. Jenney and Mr. Hudson."

Cannon used his prison time well by working on a biography of Joseph Smith, writing magazine articles, organizing a Sunday School, and teaching a Bible class. He was released from prison on February 21, 1889.[20]

▽ **George Q. Cannon, on left, and President Wilford Woodruff, at right, fishing at San Diego, California in 1889**

Wilford Woodruff was a longtime fan of fly-fishing. As early as 1847 he recorded in his journal: "I went & flung my fly onto the [water] And it being the first time that I ever tried the Artificial fly in America, . . . I watched it as it floated upon the water with as much intens interest As Franklin did his kite when tried to draw lightning from the skies. And as Franklin received great Joy when he saw electricity . . . descend on his kite string in like manner was I highly gratifyd when I saw the nimble trout dart my fly hook himself & run away with the line but I soon worried him out & drew him to shore."[21]

△ **John Burrup (1863–1929) and daughter Mary (Fox), at an Ogden, Utah, studio, ca. 1889**

John Burrup married Mary Elizabeth Quigley in Ogden in 1885. Unfortunately, she died two days short of their first wedding anniversary, leaving Burrup with an infant daughter to care for. John's own mother had died eight days after his birth. Like John, her father, young Mary was "farmed out" to be reared until he could remarry. In John's case, he married Elsie "Ella" Shurtliff in 1890, and they reared a large family in Grant, Idaho, where he homesteaded and served as a counselor in the bishopric.[22]

◁ **William F. Rigby (1833–1901) and family, Teton Basin, Alta, Wyoming, 1890**

Front row, left to right: Elmer E., Willard, and Eva and Ella, twins.

Back row: Lavinia Rigby Card, young Lavinia, Mary Card, Samuel, Zina, William, Sophia, David, Henry, James, Martha, and Emma Rigby.

William Rigby, an 1848 convert and an 1856 emigrant from England, settled in the Teton Valley in 1890 with his plural wife Sophie Eckersley Rigby (1848–1928) and their children after he served time for polygamy in the Utah Territory Penitentiary. As his granddaughter Edith Rigby Cooley relates: "This was the first home of Sophia and Wm. F. Rigby, Sr. It was built on Sophia's homestead in Alta, Wyoming in Teton Basin. It was one large room and shanty, more stylishly known as a summer kitchen. There were shelves in one end on which the children slept with their mother's good, warm, home-made quilts to cover them. These shelves would be about like bunk beds of today. They used a ladder to climb up to them. When Wm. F. Sr. came from the penitentiary, he was instructed to choose one wife but grandfather said he loved all his wives and all his children. In order to live within the law as near as possible he established homes for his wives in different localities. He took Sophia just over the line into Wyoming and built this home in Alta, Wyoming."[24]

▷ **Brigham Young, Jr., president of the British Mission, at the Giant's Causeway, Ireland, 1890**

President Brigham Young, Jr., is third from the right on the back row. Unfortunately, none of the other people are identified. In a priesthood meeting on Saturday, November 29, 1890, in Belfast, Brigham Young, Jr., told his missionaries "to listen to the dictates of the spirit of God and follow promptings. He advised them to make friends if they could not make converts, and in so doing they would be able to allay a great deal of the prejudice existing towards the Latter-day Saints."

Ireland was a hard sell. The statistical report for the end of 1890 for Ireland read: "55 members in the Irish Mission, 1 branch, 2 high Priests, 6 Seventies, 5 Elders, 3 Priests, 1 teacher, and 2 deacons. Elders Alma Hale and J. B. Jardine continued labors in Co. Armagh but with little success."[23]

Lee

WISHING YOU A MERRY CHRISTMAS AND A HAPPY NEW YEAR.

Lansdowne Portrush

△ **Laying of the capstone, Salt Lake Temple, April 6, 1892**

The building of the Salt Lake Temple began with the groundbreaking on February 14, 1853. For the Saints it was an effort filled with sacrifice, commitment, and perseverance.

President Wilford Woodruff reported in his journal: "This was the Most interesting day in some respects the Church has Ever Seen since its organization. The Temple Cap Stone was laid with imposing Ceremonies with Electricity by President Wilford Woodruff. It was Judged there was 50,000 on the Temple Grounds. . . . Before the Close

F. M. Lyman steped to the front of the Platform And said [']six months ago President Woodruff Expressed . . . that He desired to Live to See the Dedication of this Temple. It was the feelings in the Harts of the Brethren that an Effort should be made to Accomplish that work. Next April it will be 40 years from the time of the laying of the Cornor Stone of this Temple

And I have a Resolution to offer to Assembled Israel to day. . . . That this Assembly pledge themselves individually and Collectively to furnish as far as it may be Needed all Money that may be necessary to Complete the Temple at Earliest time possible so that the Dedication

may take place April 6, 1893.['] This was accepted with an uplifting of hands with a great shout. Brother Lyman Donated $1,000."[25]

◁ The crowd on Temple Block at the time of the capstone-laying ceremonies, 1892[26]

◁ Construction workers in the uncompleted Assembly Room of the Salt Lake Temple, 1892

Every endeavor was made to ensure that the Salt Lake Temple would be completed for the dedication on April 6, 1893. There was great concern to meet this goal, as reflected by President Woodruff's words: "[February 8, 1893] I . . . Met [with] the Temple Committee and several Contractors. We talked plain to all parties and they agreed to take hold & all do all they Could to finish the Temple."[27]

◁ **Temple electrician Ephraim G. Holding (1849–1927) atop the northeast finial of the Salt Lake Temple, 1893**

Ephraim Holding was born in England in 1849 and emigrated to Utah with his family in 1853. For him, the wagon trek west was more than the usual adventure, as "the Indians were very troublesome, they stole the children's clothing and food and they tried to get Grand father's [Daniel Holding, Ephraim's father] watch and chain. He refused them as it was given to [him] by his father Richard Holding when he left England; so the Indian snatched Ephraim George Holding and started off . . . and all the children screamed and cried so his father conceded to let them have his watch and got his little boy back."[28]

△ **The First Presidency, April 6, 1893, the day of the Salt Lake Temple dedication**

Left to right: George Q. Cannon, Wilford Woodruff, and Joseph F. Smith.

From President Wilford Woodruff's journal: "The dedication of the Temple Commenced at 10 oclock. Near 3,000 Assembled at the upper room. I attended the Dedication of the Temple. The spirit & Power of God rested upon us. The spirit of Prophesy & Revelation was upon us & the Hearts of the People were Melted and many thing[s] wer[e] unfolded to us. We Met in the Afternoon at 2 oclk & we had a glorious time. Woodruff & G Q Cannon and J F Smith occupied most of the time. W Woodruff offered up the prayer in the forenoon & G C Cannon in the Afternoon."[29]

△ Manti Scandinavian Choir

Logan, Salt Lake City, and Manti each had Scandinavian choirs. These choirs entertained throughout the territory: at Salt Lake City during the temple dedication, at Garfield Beach on the Great Salt Lake, at musical festivals, and at the Scandinavian Jubilee in 1900.[30]

◁ Photograph of Joseph F. Smith (1838–1918) by Salt Lake City pioneer photographer Charles R. Savage, ca. 1893

On December 25, 1893, President Joseph F. Smith presented this portrait to an aunt and good naturedly wrote the following on the back:

*"In 'underground days,' as the
    saying goes
The great C. R. Savage kindly
    proposed
To take my photograph in modern
    pose*

*I gladly consented the Savage to
    meet
And sit for my picture expecting a
    treat;
To my disappointment, as you may
    suppose
Instead of my features he photoed
    my nose!
True my whiskers came in for a
    liberal stare,
In the picture before you, as you
    will declare,
But then you'll agree with my wail
    of despair
T'was a Savage act on the part
    of C. R.
To photograph only my nose and
    my hair!"[31]*

▷ **David O. McKay (1873–1970) and the 1894 University of Utah football team**

Top row, left to right: Paul Kimball, David O. McKay, F. N. Poulson, Bernard Stewart, I. E. Wiley, and Theodore Nystrum.

Middle row: Ernest Van Cott, Fred W. Reynolds, Alonzo E. Hyde, and Joseph W. Stringfellow.

Bottom row: A. B. Sawyer, Fred J. Mays, Harry Kimball, Fred Earls, and Seth Thomas.[32]

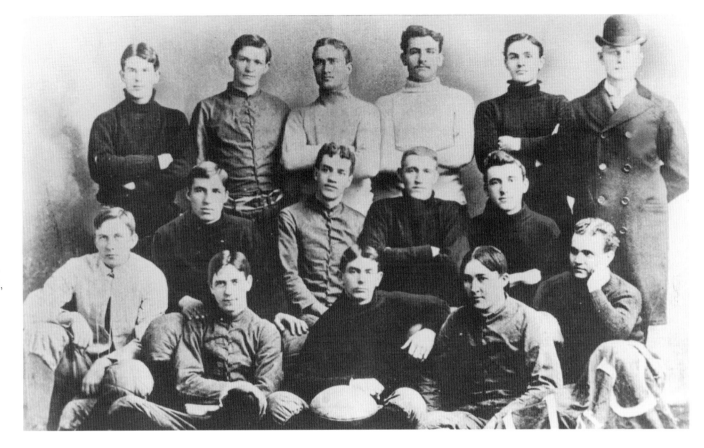

▷ **National suffragist Susan B. Anthony with Mormon and Intermountain women suffrage leaders, Salt Lake City, 1895**

Front row, left to right: Zina D. H. Young, Reverend Anna Howard Shaw, Susan B. Anthony, Sarah M. Kimball (then president of the Utah Women's Suffrage Association), and Lyle Meredith Stansbury (of Denver).

Back row: Mary C. C. Bradford (Denver), Margaret A. Caine, Electa Bullock, Dr. Martha Hughes Cannon, Phoebe Y. Beattie, Emily S. Richards, Emmeline B. Wells, Rebecca M. Little, and Augusta W. Grant.

This photograph was taken in May 1895 following the successful franchise campaign that ended on April 18, 1895, when the Utah Constitutional Convention voted to include universal suffrage into the Utah State Constitution. The nineteenth amendment to the United States Constitution (giving women the right to vote) was not passed until August 26, 1920.[33]

▽ **Midwife class in Salt Lake City, 1896**

Portrait of unidentified students with their teacher, Dr. Ellis R. Shipp (1847–1939), who is seated farthest right in the middle row.

Dr. Shipp was an 1878 graduate of Woman's Medical College of Pennsylvania, a staff member of the Deseret Hospital, founder of a school of nursing and obstetrics, co-editor of a pioneer medical journal, member of the Relief Society General Board, president of the Utah Women's Press Club, and a delegate to the National Council of Women in Washington, D.C.

Dr. Ralph T. Richards wrote in his book *Of Medicine, Hospitals, and Doctors:* "Dr. Ellis R. Shipp's great contribution to the welfare of the women of Utah and the Intermountain West was made by conducting systematic, thorough, and complete instruction classes in nursing and obstetrics. She was kind, considerate, and patient with her pupils, but she never gave a certificate of graduation to any student who did not have the mental and personal qualifications necessary to make a good, practical nurse and midwife."[34]

△ **Missionaries with the James Giles family, Lifuke, Tonga, 1895**

Standing, back row, left to right: Elder Thomas Adams, Elder William P. Hunter, and Elder Albert S. Jones.

Front row: Ellen Giles, Emma Giles, Racheal Giles, James E. Giles, Louisa Giles, and George Giles.

James Giles was an influential Englishman living in Tonga when Elders Hunter and Adams baptized him in October 1894.[35]

◁ **Salt Lake Tabernacle decorated for Utah statehood celebration, 1896**

On January 4, 1896, a young lawyer by the name of Charles B. Stewart (1870–1945) noted in his diary: "UTAH IS A STATE AT LAST. It was proclaimed a state in Washington at noon today. Forty-nine years our fathers have been in serfdom and vassalage, have been persecuted and driven, but today, AT LAST, we enjoy the freedom of true Americans. We enjoy the freedom designed by our great Creator to be the lot of every child beneath the blue sky. Great God, we praise thy name in so moving the minds of men to secure our liberty. Happy indeed we are, with beating hearts of gratitude and joy. All the whistles are blowing, the bells ringing, guns firing, and the people are blowing trumpets and shouting loud for joy. My sweet girl Kate, and I walked up and across City Creek and thence downtown to see the throngs of people wild with delight. [January 6, 1896.] Everybody from all over the State here celebrating. . . . Great procession downtown, and services in the Tabernacle amid flags, bunting, flowers, etc. A flag hung from the ceiling 128 x 150'."[36]

△ **Crowd at the statehood parade, west side of Main Street between South Temple and First South, Salt Lake City, January 6, 1896**[37]

◁ **Robert T. Burton (1821–1907), Marshall of the Day, Statehood Day, January 6, 1896**

When he was honored by being made the "Marshall of the Day," Robert T. Burton was seventy-five years old and the first counselor in the Presiding Bishopric. He had served in the Nauvoo Legion and in the Nauvoo Legion Brass Band, participated in Utah's early Indian conflicts, served as an officer in the Utah Nauvoo Legion (reaching the rank of major general), and helped with the rescue of the stranded handcart companies of 1856. In addition to his military offices and frontier experience, citizen Burton was also at various times a constable of Salt Lake City, deputy territorial marshall, and a member of the Salt Lake City Council.

A proud family stated of his participation in the statehood celebrations: "He did it so well we were awfully proud of him, that he could sit up as straight as he did because he was then what was considered an old man."[38]

▷ **Salt Lake Temple draped with the statehood flag, 1896**[39]

△ **Elders A. T. Rose and George Moroni Fryer, Port Gibson, Mississippi, 1897**

Derbies, Prince Albert coats, umbrellas, and satchels—typical outfits of Mormon missionaries in the States and Europe.[40]

▽ **Baptism, Samoan Mission, ca. 1896**

Mission President Edward J. Wood (1866–1956), who, on his second mission to Samoa, described his tracting experience on the island of Savai'i in January 1896: "A long walk with nothing to eat, and [we] finally get rained on. It's a long walk at the best, but when it rains it is something horrible. We walked about 8 miles through the bushes while it simply poured down, and . . . we had no [extra] clothes so after arriving at Aopu we had to sit and wait for our clothes to dry. . . . This is the poorest village for hospitality I ever saw. No body came to see us but some forward-looking girls and all we had to eat was a small breadfruit each and that was all we had all day, but the Lord made it sweet to our taste." But two months later he reported better news: "Siupapa Sunday Mch 7. . . . To day was surely a red letter day for us. We had the privilege of baptizing twelve into the church."[41]

◁ **Mormon Battalion members at the fiftieth anniversary celebration of the discovery of gold, San Francisco, January 1898**

Left to right: Henry W. Bigler, William J. Johnston, Azariah Smith, and James S. Brown.

All of these gentlemen were at Sutter's Mill, California, when gold was discovered on January 24, 1848. Bigler is credited with recording the event: "My journal tells me it was on the afternoon of the twenty-fourth day of January, 1848, . . . when Marshall as usual went to see Wimmer and the Indians who were at work towards the lower end of the race. Then he sent a young Indian for Brown to send him a plate. . . . Just before we quit work, he [Marshall] came up and said he believed he had found a gold mine. . . . The next morning . . . every man at his own job, Marshall came up carrying his old white hat in his arms looking wonderfully pleased and good natured. There was a heavy smile on his countenance. . . . As he came up he said, 'Boys, by G_d I believe I have found a gold mine' and set his hat on the work bench that stood in the mill yard. Every man gathered instantly around to see what he had and there, sure enough, on the top of the hat crown (knocked in a little) lay the pure stuff."[42]

▽ **Quarterly conference, Relief Society, San Juan Stake, Utah, ca. 1898**

Front row, left to right: Mary Nielsen Jones, Harriet Barton Hammond, Aggie Allen Pearson, Jennie Decker Wood, Ann Bayles, Annie Decker Wood, Caroline Hammond, Sarah Perkins, and, standing to the side, Sister Sorensen, teacher.

Middle row: Josephine Wood, Cornelia Mortensen, Annette Nielson Johnson, Celestia Stevens Hancock, Marion Brunson, Lucinda A. Redd, Caroline Nielson Redd, Corry Perkins, Celestia Hammond, and Lettie Stephens Jensen.

Back row: Lydia May Lyman Jones, Evelyn Adams, Emma Scarup, Elza A. Redd, Annie M. Decker, M. M. Halls (from Moncos, Colorado), Adelia Lyman, and Evelyn Lyman Bayles.

Living away from more populated areas in a relatively desolate area, where families made their living from the land, an important and continual message among the San Juan Stake Relief Societies was for "mothers to teach girls to be self sustaining and not wait for a man who is able to keep them in ease and luxury."[43]

△ **Three generations: mother, son, and granddaughter, 1899**

Left to right: Martha Silcock Pixton (1852–1916), Martha Naomi Pixton (1898–1994), and Seth Silcock Pixton (1875–1956).

Born at Granstville in 1852, Martha Pixton, wife of Robert Pixton, was widowed at the age of twenty-nine. While raising her three children alone, she served as the second president of the Riverton Ward Primary and, later, the ward's Relief Society treasurer. She said of her life: "[I] knew nothing but pioneer life and underwent privation in connection with my parents and brothers and sisters. . . . My education was very limited in book learning, but rich in the school of experience."[44]

▽ **Madame Nellie Melba (1861–1931) performing in the Salt Lake Tabernacle, April 15, 1898**

Nellie Melba appeared with the Tabernacle Choir even though she harbored the ill feelings toward the Church that were common at the time. However, choir conductor Evan Stephens was able to soften her opinion.

Of Melba's concert the *Deseret Evening News* reported: "The appearance of Madame Melba at the Tabernacle last night adds another notable achievement to the long list of important events which this historic old building can already boast. . . . The greatest of interest has been taken, for the last month, in the appearance there of Madame Melba, the Australian songstress, because of the fact that she is considered by eminent critics the queen of the lyric stage at the present time. Not to have heard a noted artist like Melba is considered a serious mistake, for it will form the leading topic of conversation in social circles for a long time to come."[45]

MELBA IN THE MORMON TABERNACLE. ABL.15ᵗʰ 1898.

JOHNSON PHOTO.

△ Funeral of Wilford Woodruff, Salt Lake Tabernacle, September 8, 1898

In 1882 Wilford Woodruff wrote instructions involving his burial: "I do not wish any black made use of about my coffin, or about the vehicle that conveys my body to the grave. I do not wish my family or friends to wear any badge of mourning for me at my funeral or afterwards, for, if I am true and faithful unto death, there will be no necessity for any one to mourn for me. I have no directions to give concerning the services of my funeral, any further than it would be pleasing to me for as many of the Presidency and Twelve Apostles who may be present to speak as may be thought wisdom. Their speech will be to the living. If the laws and customs of the spirit world will permit, I should wish to attend my funeral myself, but I shall be governed by the counsel I receive in the spirit world."[46]

▷ Wilford Woodruff's funeral procession, Salt Lake City, September 8, 1898

The procession is moving east along South Temple Street, in front of the Lion House and Beehive House, toward the Salt Lake City Cemetery.[47]

▷ **David D. Rust (1874–1963) (at tent opening) and his brother Bill (1867–1952) camping in southern Utah, 1899**

David Rust was one of the earliest Colorado River boatmen and guides. He extensively explored the Colorado River and surrounding areas. He guided many hunting, fishing, and touring groups through the wilds of southern Utah and northern Arizona. Some of his better-known clients were Theodore Roosevelt, Zane Grey, Utah governor George Dern, and scientific groups from the Peabody Museum of Harvard University.

However, Rust was not a "one-trick pony." He was educated at Brigham Young University and Stanford University. He taught school, served as superintendent of Kane County School District, was Mayor of Kanab, and served in the Utah State Legislature in both the senate and the house.

As for his love of the wild landscape of southern Utah, he stated: "I have failed if I fail to assist you to love my country. I count whatever money I may receive from any group of travelers as nothing, absolutely nothing, less than nothing, if they do not leave these breaks loving these gorges, these painted cliffs, and these dusty deserts."[48]

◁ **David Rust and his students, Hanksville School, 1899**[49]

STATE SENATOR

589 K. MATTIE HUGHES CANNON. 1899.

◁ **Utah State senator Martha Hughes Cannon (1857–1932) and her daughter Gwendolyn, 1899**

Mattie Cannon was an 1880 graduate of the University of Michigan Medical School and an 1882 graduate of the University of Pennsylvania and the National School for Elocution and Oratory. In 1884 Mattie became the plural wife of Angus M. Cannon and soon thereafter set up a private medical practice and taught classes in nursing and obstetrics. Mattie and Angus were the parents of three children. Her political interests led to her involvement in the suffragist movement, and in 1896 she became the first woman in the United States to be elected a state senator. Her political and medical careers mixed when she served on Utah's first state board of health, which was created from a bill she introduced during her first term in the state senate. Her ongoing concern for public health motivated Dr. Cannon to lead a successful effort to abolish the use of tin cups that were chained to the drinking fountains.[50]

MUTUAL IMPROVEMENT ASSOCIATION MISSIONARIES. 1899-1900.

◁ **Lorenzo Snow speaking in the Box Elder Tabernacle at the funeral of Alvin Nichols, September 1899**[51]

△ **Mutual Improvement Association Missionaries, 1899**

These missionaries were sent to work with local stake, ward, and branch leadership of the MIA and to aid them to "be not satisfied, rest not content, until every young man professing the name of saint in Zion is enrolled in the cause of Mutual Improvement."[52]

▷ **"Company 6" of the Big Horn Basin settlers crossing Hams Fork near Kemmerer, Wyoming, 1900**

In early April 1900, President Lorenzo Snow appointed Elder Abraham O. Woodruff to be in charge of Church members willing to colonize the Big Horn Basin. The colonizers met at Hams Fork near Kemmerer, Wyoming, on April 25, 1900. These Saints gathered from Salt Lake, Bountiful, Morgan, Woodruff, Evanston, and Bear Lake. The more than 250 men, women, and children were divided into seven companies. The last company left Hams Fork on May 3, 1900, and arrived in the Big Horn Basin on May 24, 1900.

On May 28 the newly arrived settlers met by the Shoshone River to dedicate the land and the canals they were about to build. Elder Abraham Woodruff said in his remarks: "The canal will be 37 miles long and must be large enough to carry the water to irrigate from twelve to fifteen thousand acres of land. The work has not begun, but it will start tomorrow. . . . I urge you to keep the Word of Wisdom, pay your tithes, and offerings. Do not profane the name of Deity. Be honest with all men. Honor the Sabbath day and if you do these things, this will be a land of Zion unto you and your children and children's children throughout the generations that are to come."[53]

▷ **Montage of individual portraits of the First Presidency and the Quorum of Twelve Apostles, 1900**[54]

△ **Sacrament service, Ephraim Tabernacle, ca. 1900**

At the table, left to right: Mons Nielson, Peter Isaacson, and Andrew Thompson, Jr. On the stand at left is Knute Peterson.

The painting of Joseph Smith receiving the gold plates is by C.C.A. Christensen.[55]

◁ **President Lorenzo Snow (1814–1901) in the Salt Lake Temple, ca. 1901**

A Reverend Prentis, visiting from North Carolina in 1898, reported: "I had expected to find intellect, intellectuality, benevolence, dignity, composure and strength depicted upon the face of the President of the Church of Jesus Christ of Latter-day Saints; but when I was introduced to Pres. Lorenzo Snow for a second I was startled to see the holiest face but one I had ever been privileged to look upon. His face was a poem of peace, his presence a benediction of peace. In the tranquil depths of his eyes were the 'home of silent prayer' and the abode of spiritual strength. . . . The picture of that slight, venerable form hallowed with the aura of an ineffable peace will haunt my heart like the vision of a celestial picture."[56]

◁ **Missionaries and wives in Japan, ca. 1902**

Seated, left to right: Mary Grant (Judd) (daughter of Augusta and Heber J. Grant), Augusta W. Grant, Mrs. Joseph F. Featherstone, and Mamie W. Ensign.

Standing: Alma O. Taylor, Erastus L. Jarvis, John W. Stoker, Fred A. Caine, Apostle Heber J. Grant, Sanford W. Hedges, Horace S. Ensign, and Joseph F. Featherstone.

Apostle Heber J. Grant dedicated Japan for the preaching of the gospel in the fall of 1901. Elder Alma Taylor reported: "Brother Grant offered up the dedicatory prayer. His tongue was loosened and the spirit rested mightily upon him; so much so that we felt that the angels of God were near for our hearts burned within us as the words fell from his lips. I never experienced such a peaceful influence or heard such a powerful prayer before; every word penetrated into my very bones and I could have wept with joy."[1]

△ **Provo Fourth Ward Band, 1902**

Front row, left to right: Franklyn Y. Gates, William E. Bassett, Vivian Snow, Irving Snow, Jesse Fields, and Harold Smoot.

Back row: Calvin Beebe, Leonard Cluff, B. Cecil Gates, Karl Keeler, Ray Warner, Jesse Haws, Harvey H. Gates, Elwood Beebe, and Wilford Smoot.

In 1978 Vivian Snow told how the Provo Fourth Ward band was formed: "In the spring of 1900 a few of the youngsters living in the Provo Fourth Ward met on the lawn in front of Uncle Jacob Gate's home to make plans for the upcoming summer. After much talk and arguing we decided to have a circus. . . . Our progress was very slow, so when someone said, 'If we are going to have a circus we should have a band,'

this suggestion took fire. . . . A few of the boys had instruments and we were able to recruit thirteen who either had instruments or who would buy them. Irving Snow was made leader . . . but we had professional instruction until we were able to play three marches. The first teacher was Prof. Albert Miller . . . [of] Brigham Young Academy and then later, William Holdaway, trombone player with the Provo City Band. The band was

invited to play at a Fourth of July celebration in the Provo Tabernacle. . . . We thought we received as much applause as did the B.Y.A. band. The band was together until the latter part of 1903 when the Gates family moved to Salt Lake City. . . . Harold Smoot moved to Washington, his father, Reed Smoot, having been elected to the U.S. Senate."[2]

◁ **United States president Theodore Roosevelt in Salt Lake City, 1903**

On the day of Theodore Roosevelt's visit to Utah, Apostle John Henry Smith noted in his diary: "[Tuesday, May 19, 1903] President Theodore Roosevelt and Associates reached here this morning. Hundreds of men, women and children turned out to meet him. He spoke to the school children at the city Hall and to the people in the Tabernacle. He had breakfast at Senator Thomas Kearns. He left Salt Lake City about 1:30 P.M. He received me with open arms as an old time friend."

Theodore Roosevelt was the first U.S. President to speak in the Tabernacle and to publicly speak favorably of the Mormons.[3]

▷ **Ella Wheeler Wilcox (1850–1919) with Mormon women, Saltair, 1903.**

Front and center in this picture is Ella Wheeler Wilcox, then a world famous writer and poetess.

Front row, left to right: unidentified, unidentified, Elder Charles W. Penrose, Emmeline B. Wells, Ida Smoot Dusenbury, and Mrs. Fox Young.

Second row: unidentified, Romania Pratt Penrose, unidentified, Lula Green Richards, Annie Taylor Hyde, unidentified, and Phoebe Y. Beattie.

Third row: Are all unidentified, except on the far left is Margaret Nightingale Caine, and on the far right is Dr. Martha Hughes Cannon.

For many years Ella Wheeler Wilcox wrote a daily poem for a syndicated newspaper column, and she published more than twenty volumes of verse, including *Drops of Water* (1872), *Poems of Passion* (1883), and *The Art of Being Alive* (1914). In her 1918 autobiography, *The Worlds and I,* she said of her visit to Utah: "A day in Salt Lake City, Utah, I have never forgotten, where I went out to see the remains of the Salt Sea, in company with twenty-two women who had all been polygamous wives. One Elder accompanied the party; and he had been, until the laws of the Government made polygamy unconstitutional, the happy husband of six wives. He talked to me freely of their ideals, and the deeply religious sentiment on which Mormonism was founded. . . . At the end of what was a very interesting afternoon, I was photographed with the party of Mormon women and the Elder."[4]

▷ **Old Folks Day excursion, American Fork, Utah, June 30, 1903**

Pioneer photographer Charles R. Savage (1831–1909) is seated next to the tree.

Next to Savage, left to right: unidentified, Joseph R. Morgan, William Jones, D. M. McAllister, William Brown, William H. Foster, and Ebenezer Beesley with violin.

Old Folks Day was begun by Charles Savage (with the help of Bishop Edward Hunter and George Goddard) in 1875 as a way to honor pioneers by providing an annual recreational outing for those seventy years of age and older. According to Savage family records, "Whenever Mr. Savage would pass [John Daynes'] house, he would see John's elderly mother sitting on the porch. She was there day after day, . . . and Savage wondered if she ever went outside of the yard. He thought that there must be other old people that lived in the same way, and the idea came to him that it would be a fine thing to give all elderly people an outing once a year."

These outings continued for several decades after the founders' deaths. Tribute was

paid to Savage in 1936 when a monument, capped with a sculpted bronze bust of him, was placed on the southeast corner of Temple Square block in downtown Salt Lake City. The inscription on the memorial reads:

In Affectionate Remembrance of Charles R. Savage and In Reverential regard for the Old Folks whose happiness He so greatly promoted Through the establishment of Old folks day in Utah.[5]

△ First Presidency, 1904

Left to right: President Joseph F. Smith (1838–1918), Anthon H. Lund (1844–1921), second counselor, and John R. Winder (1821–1910), first counselor.[6]

▽ **Midwife "Aunt Jody" (Josephine Catherine Chatterly Wood, 1853–1909), Bluff, Utah, ca. 1905**

The lack (and sometimes distrust) of doctors made midwives essential to health on the frontier. Aunt Jody attended the families of southeast Utah, from Bluff to Monticello, for more than twenty years. Shortly after arriving in the Bluff area with her family in the 1880s, she was called to be a midwife by Bishop Jense Nielson—she had no experience, but the bishop and his counselors felt she would learn and "do it"; she was highly educated from experience gained in the university of the frontier. Her daughter Catherine Hansen stated: "When the first call came for a confinement case, Mother was afraid. My father blessed her, asking the Lord to guide her and give her wisdom for any emergency she might have to meet. In this he was setting a precedent for many occasions of the future. Ofttimes the whole family knelt in prayer for Mother as she went forth on her mission of mercy."[7]

◁ **Picnic at John McDonald's summer home, Salt Lake City, 1905**

In attendance at this picnic were many General Authorities, including President Joseph F. Smith, Anthon H. Lund, B. H. Roberts, Charles Penrose, John R. Winder, Francis M. Lyman, John Henry Smith, Hyrum M. Smith, and Rudger Clawson. This home was later destroyed by fire. John McDonald (1830–1910) was a pioneer and successful confectionery merchant.[8]

▷ **General conference crowd, Temple Square, Salt Lake City, Utah, April 6, 1906**[9]

▷ **Pioneer photographer Charles R. Savage at home, Salt Lake City, Christmas, 1905**

Charles Roscoe Savage was born in England in 1832 and converted to Mormonism there in 1848. Upon his emigration to New York City in 1856, he learned everything he could about the new profession he had chosen—photography. Savage arrived in Salt Lake City in 1860 and immediately opened a photographic business, first in partnership with Marsena Cannon, then with artist George Ottinger. After 1872 Savage was the sole proprietor of his business. Savage was a major pioneer photographer, respected and sought out by his peers. He photographically documented the growth and development of Salt Lake City and vicinity. Many Utah residents, government officials, and LDS Church leaders appeared in front of Savage's camera. However, he was perhaps at his best when photographing the landscapes of the West. During his professional career, which spanned nearly fifty years, he won first prizes for his photograph exhibits at the World Expositions in Chicago, St. Louis, San Francisco, and

Portland. An active member of the Church and community, he was a member of the Tabernacle Choir, served on the Salt Lake Stake high council, and was a captain in the Utah Nauvoo Legion. He died in 1909.[10]

△ Heber J. Grant and wife, Emily Wells Grant, in St. Mark's Square, Venice, Italy, spring 1906

At the time of this photograph, Apostle Heber J. Grant was the president of the European Mission. While touring Italy, he wrote: "Never have I been more profoundly impressed with deep gratitude for the gospel than since I came on this trip; and this trip to Rome . . . has increased this feeling. The simplicity of the gospel in comparison with the display [of Italy and Europe] has never been made so forcible to my mind. I would not have missed this trip for anything."[11]

△ **Pioneer Stake Primary Board**, Salt Lake City, Utah, **1907**

Front row, left to right: Annie L. Poulton, Rose Cannon Lambert, Edith Hunter (president), Olive Pixton Eardley, and Pearl Tomlinson.

Back row: Edith McClelland, Annie Jorgensen, Grace Cannon Neslen, and Nora Hunter Barton.

This photograph was taken in August 1907 prior to President Edith Hunter's September departure for a mission to the Sandwich Islands

(Hawaii). She is wearing the gold chain and locket that her Primary board gave her as a going-away gift.[12]

▷ **Fun in San Francisco, ca. 1908**

Left to right: President Joseph F. Smith, John Henry Smith, and Sarah Ellen Richards Smith (wife of Joseph F. Smith, 1850–1915).[13]

◁ **Party for Sister Edith Hunter, Liberty Park, Salt Lake City, July 27, 1910**

Edith Hunter returned home from her mission to the Sandwich Islands on July 22, 1910. Her friends gathered at Liberty Park for a party to welcome her back to Salt Lake City. Edith Hunter (1878–1964) served on the general board of the Primary Association from 1910 to 1939, and for twenty-seven years she was resident director at the LDS Hospital Nurses' Home. In 1915 she married James N. Lambert, and together they raised three children.[14]

◁ **Kofu, Japan, Sunday School class taught by Joseph H. Stimpson, October 11, 1908**

Elder Joseph H. Stimpson (1885–1964) wrote in his diary: "Sunday, October 11th, 1908. . . . Arose at 7. Prepared my room. Ate. We had a very nice school though small. My class took very good part. We had Mark 5:21–43. Ate soon after school and after taking a picture of my class. We had Sacrament Meeting at 1:00. Talked after. At 3 a fairly good attendance came to Bible Class. After class I read. Supper over we played some flute-violin duetts. Our Preaching meeting began nearly on time. 13 were present. The subject was 'Life and Environment.' After meeting we talked for some time with Misses Iso and Shioiri. Retired a short time later—after some discussion of our trip to Tokyo next week and the best possible route to take for it."[15]

△ **Marie Hermansen's dining room, Aarhus, Denmark, ca. 1910**

Left to right: Thomas Hermansen, Elder Arthur Nielsen, Elder Orson Garff, Marie Hermansen, and President Andrew Andersen.

Mr. Hermansen enjoyed entertaining Mormon missionaries from the United States. He liked to practice his English, and he sought the latest news of America.[16]

▷ **Howard W. Hunter (1907–1995), age two**

The son of Nellie Rasmussen and John W. Hunter. He became the fourteenth president of the Church.[17]

▷ Salt Lake Temple, ca. 1911[18]

▷ **Mormon refugee tent city, El Paso, Texas, 1912**

During the Mexican revolution, the Saints living in the Mexican colonies were forced to flee across the border into the United States. These Saints lived in a tent city set up in El Paso, Texas, by the United States government. The government also helped provide food and some clothing.

In August 1912, Orrin P. Miller, first counselor in the Presiding Bishopric, reported: "I arrived at El Paso at 5:12 last evening. . . . I visited the refugees late in the evening and found a condition that was most appalling. Quite a number of women and children were ill; several infants had been born en route and since the arrival at El Paso. The committee was successful in getting 150 moved last evening to the St. Joseph Stake. . . . The government is purchasing some supplies and the people of El Paso have been very liberal with their means and have rendered very valuable assistance. . . . The sight presented to my view is one of the most heart-rending I have ever witnessed—to see over 2,000 people, mostly women and children, driven from their homes without time to gather even their personal effects and most of them without a dollar to assist themselves with. . . . We are expecting 500 tents from the government today."

Prior to the exodus, the local Mormon leaders made a valiant effort to work out a peaceful coexistence with the Mexican revolutionaries, but the chaos and uncertainties created by the warring factions forced the abandonment of the colonies the Saints had worked so hard to create and maintain. Colonia Diaz was burned during the revolution. No attempt was made to recolonize Colonia Morelos after the revolution. The effort to resettle the colonies of Pacheco, Garcia, and Chuichupa proved unsuccessful. However, colonias Juarez and Dublan were successfully repopulated and still exist to this day.[19]

◁ **Orson D. Romney (1860–1941), with Maori family, Auckland, New Zealand, 1912**

Mission president Orson Romney was serving his second mission to New Zealand when this image was taken. His first mission was from 1888 to 1892. On the back of the photograph Elder Romney wrote: "Sitting with some Elders and a Maori family just before morning prayer around some red hot coals in a pan as it was quite cold that morning. You will notice I am sitting on a box and David to my right reading. That little Maori boy looking straight ahead—you ought to hear him pray as few men can."[20]

▷ **Physical education class, Brigham Young University, 1911**[21]

▽ **Men's exercise group at the old Deseret Gym, Salt Lake City, 1913**

Front row: (1) Verden A. Bettilyon, (2) David A. Smith, (3) W. R. Hurst, (4) William Service, (5) Robert H. Siddoway, (6) Allen E. Park, (7) John Fetzer, (8) Harold W. Ansell, (9) Frank W. Beeraft, (10) Herbert Hirschman, and (11) O.P.J. Widtsoe.

Middle row: (1) George J. Cannon, (2) Albert D. McMullen, (3) John D. Giles, (4) Charles Gibbs, (5) Stephen L Richards, (6) Adrian B. Pembroke, (7) James N. Lambert, (8) Harold G. Reynolds, (9) W. Scott Groo, (10) Andrew A. Gladd, and (11) William E. Day, instructor.

Back row: (1) Mr. Mosher, (2) Feremorz Y. Fox, (3) E. L. Sloan, (4) Heber J. Grant, (5) John H. Taylor, (6) Lorenzo Jensen, (7) Tom Lambert, (8) Leo H. Young, (9) Howard Dalton, (10) Bryant S. Hinckley, (11) Hyrum S. Welling, (12) unidentified, (13) General Richard W. Young, (14) George C. Lambert, (15) A. William Lund, (16) Roy L. Williams, (17) Joseph Fielding Smith, (18) William G. Lambert, and (19) O. Spencer Squires.[22]

◁ **Newlyweds William Edward Burrup and Elizabeth Fox Burrup, April 4, 1907**

This young married couple decorated themselves with lilacs they picked while walking from the Salt Lake Temple to the photographer's studio. The day before their wedding, the couple hailed a train near Downata Hot Springs by building a fire near the railroad tracks. When the train stopped, the couple boarded with Elizabeth's widowed mother, Margaret G. Fox, and journeyed 120 miles to Salt Lake City. After their marriage, they homesteaded in Idaho. Their first child was born in 1908, a daughter named Virgil. Because of their distressed financial circumstances at the time, the Burrups were unable to buy a dress for baby Virgil to be blessed in. Elizabeth, with willing but heavy heart, took scissors, needle, and thread and transformed the skirt of her wedding dress into a beautiful baby gown in which Virgil was blessed. The gown was subsequently used by all of the couple's six children.[23]

▽ **Eldest children of Ed and Bessie Burrup, 1913**

The baby gown refashioned from Bessie's wedding dress is worn by Clyde, born on Halloween 1912. His sister Virgil stands behind him, and his brother Percy stands to the side.[24]

▷ **Elder Spencer W. Kimball, missionary, Central States Mission, Pea Ridge, Missouri, ca. 1914**

Like most missionaries, Elder Spencer Kimball was at times discouraged. His father, Andrew Kimball, wrote these words of encouragement: "I am pleased with your game spirit. You will make good, Spencer. You are small in stature—so was your sweet mother—but big natured and whole souled. You will make good, my boy. Your hard experiences will enable you to know just a little of what it costs to be a Latter-day Saint and something of what your father and grandfather waded through. Keep up a good courageous spirit, but don't get to think it is too much for you to bear. It will all come out well and you will have something to tell your posterity. . . . God bless my sweet boy."[25]

◁ **Son and father, apostle and prophet, 1914**

Apostle Joseph Fielding Smith (1876–1972) and his father, the Prophet Joseph F. Smith.

Of his family Joseph F. Smith wrote: "The objects of my life become more apparent as time advances and experience grows. Those objects being the proclamation of the Gospel, or the establishment of the Kingdom of God on the earth, the salvation of souls—and most important of which to me is that of my family. The richest of all my earthly joys is in my precious children. Thank God!"[26]

▷ **Elder B. H. Roberts (1857–1933), lieutenant and chaplain of the 145th Utah Light Artillery, 1917**

Brigham Henry Roberts, seventy, historian, and theologian, wrote many volumes dealing with historical and theological themes. His books include *The Life of John Taylor, The Rise and Fall of Nauvoo, New Witness for God, Outlines of Ecclesiastical History,* and the six-volume *Comprehensive History of the Church.*

During World War I, Elder Roberts, at the age of sixty, served as the chaplain of the 145th Utah Light Artillery as they fought in France. Because

of his "sparkling sense of humor and sympathy, kindliness and dignity . . . [he] won his way with those spirited soldiers. . . . Not only their spiritual advisor, he was a father and a big brother to all of them. . . . Many a soldier . . . fearing to face the great adventure spiritually alone, gained fresh courage as this man of God charted the way for him."[27]

△ Washakie Ward Relief Society, Utah, 1918

Most of the people in this ward were of the Northwest Shoshone Native American community.

Standing, left to right: Cohn Zundel, Lewis Jones Neaman, Pasitze Norigan, Sadie Peyope, Towenga Timbimboo, Yanpatch Timbimboo, Mary Ann Ward, Helen Young (schoolteacher), Amy Timbimboo, unidentified, Ivy Hootchew Bird, Annie Hootchew, unidentified, Minnie Woonsook, Hytope Joshua,

Hazel Timbimboo Zundel (child), Joan Timbimboo Martinez (child), Minnie Zundel, and Evans Peyope.

Sitting: Poe Ne Nitz, Jane Pabwena, Mary Woonsook, Anzie Wagon, and Eddie Wagon.[28]

△ **Church leaders and families
at the Great Salt Lake, 1922**

Front row, left to right: Hyrum G.
Smith, Martha Gee Smith,
unidentified, Lucy Emily
Woodruff Smith, and Mrs. Joel
Richards.

Second row: Joseph Fielding
Smith, Ethel Reynolds Smith,
Rachael Taylor, Lucy Taylor,
unidentified, and George Albert
Smith.

Third row: James E. Talmage, his
daughter Elsie Talmage, Emily
Jenkins Smith, John H. Taylor,
John Wells, and Joel Richards.

Back row: Harold C. Brandley,
David A. Smith, and J. Golden
Kimball.[29]

▷ **Inauguration of radio station KZN, 1922**

Front row, left to right: Nathan O. Fullmer (business manager of the *Deseret News*), George Albert Smith, Augusta Winters Grant, President Heber J. Grant, Mayor C. Clarence Neslen (Salt Lake City), and George J. Cannon.

In the doorway: Anthony W. Ivins, H. C. Wilson (operator/technician) and B. F. Grant.

On the back of the photograph Nathan Fullmer wrote: "This is a flash light picture taken on the roof of the Deseret News Building—the opening (5–6–22) night of the Radio Broadcasting station KZN of the News. It being one of the most wonderful things of the age. Our station will send messages of all kinds thro the air with no wire connection of any kind, but only on the . . . waves of the atmosphere, for from 1500 miles to 2500 miles. The opening program was one of the greatest events of my life. President Grant gave the first speech of greeting to the world, then Mayor Neslen, Apostle Geo. Albert Smith, Sister Grant, Pres. Ivins, and then myself. Bro. Smith gave me a hug and said I was to be congratulated for my work. You will notice his arm around me in the picture."[30]

▷ **Missionaries in London, England, posed by an advertisement for the motion picture *Trapped by the Mormons*, ca. 1922**

Left to right: Elder Horace W. Shurtleff, unidentified, and Elder Wilford G. Edling.

The anti-Mormon movie *Trapped by the Mormons* was produced in England in 1922. It was based on the novel *A Love Story of a Mormon*, by British author and anti-Mormon crusader Winifred Graham. The movie's opening scenes zoomed in on a man's pale face and his sinister, hypnotic eyes complete with pulsating eyebrows. This image was followed with subtitles stating that the owner of the eyes "by means of his mesmeric powers is one of the cleverest recruiters in the Mormon ranks." No doubt this cinematic image did little to help the Mormon missionaries' cause. However, it is hard to think anyone could seriously believe such melodramatic stereotypes.[31]

◁ **Elders of the Eastern States Mission, Middletown, New York, ca. 1923**

Left to right: Elders Ducy, Bunker, Eldrige, Wardell, and Moore.[32]

△ **Cardston Temple choir at the Cardston Temple dedication, Alberta, Canada, August 26, 1923**

Front row, left to right: Nora A. Bullock, Vergie Olson, Lexie Burton, Blanche O. Low, Lila L. Hicken, Rose S. Henson, Rosabelle Thorpe, and Racheal N. Waneford.

Second row: Alice Baker Kraft, Lucile W. Pilling, Alma Coombs Hansen, Janie B. Wood, Hattie B. Jensen, Doris H. Pilling, Alta Hammer Thompson, and Nora Sheffield.

Third row: D. Jay Gibb, Grant Broadhead, David Gibb, George Robbins, Slyvester Low, I. M. Coombs, Edwin Leavitt, and Christen Jensen.

Top row, left to right: Ireta Head, Will Tyler, Luella S. Smith, Will Leavitt, Ibbie May, Josephine L. Allred, John Davis, John Smith, A. B. Cure, Rolly Jensen, Lavon Hudson, Ben May, Mabel Henson, W. H. Stud, Dave Rollins, Frank Layne, Dewey Smith, Annie Steed Green, and Art Henson.

Cardston Temple President Edward Wood reported in his journal: "Sunday, Aug. 26 [1923]: Yesterday the President's [Heber J. Grant's] company arrived from Salt Lake in two sleepers and a special train. . . . Thousands of visitors from every where were here. . . . President Grant offered the opening prayer Sunday morning at 10:00 A.M., August 26, 1923, at first session."[33]

▷ **President Heber J. Grant and party picnicking at Waterton Lakes, Canada, the day after the dedication of the Cardston Temple, August 30, 1923**

Apostle James E. Talmage is standing in the front and center pointing up to his right; President Heber J. Grant is standing in the front and off to our right. From Edward Wood's journal: "Thursday, the Leavitt and Mt. View Wards got up a fine picnic and went ahead of others, and we followed with 19 cars loaded down with the entire party who attended our Temple services as Church officials. We arrived [at] Waterton Lakes at 12:30 . . . , motored thru the fine streets in the pines and along the lake shores, then gathered out side Lee Nielsen's cottage for dinner. . . . We had 125 served . . . 71 trout, chickens and all kinds of meats and vegetables, cake and ice cream. . . . We hurried to the wharf on the Lake where the two launches were soon filled by our guests. . . . We never had a more pleasant ride up to the head of the Lakes and back. The many who didn't go in the boats stood on the shore and sang 'We Thank Thee, O God, For a Prophet. As our boats neared the shore Pres. Grant stood up in the boat and thanked all for kindnesses shown. It was an inspiring scene and sound."[34]

△ **Apostle David O. McKay, European Mission president, pitching horseshoes with missionary Mickey Oswald, ca. 1924**

possible sixteen) letters in football, basketball, baseball, and track at East High School in Salt Lake City. Before and after his mission, he continued this impressive record at the University of Utah, where he excelled in the same sports. After graduating from the University of Utah, he taught and coached at East High School from 1929 to 1965. He coached, of course, football, basketball, baseball, track, tennis, swimming, and skiing. He was a member of the high council of the Bonneville Stake. Later, he and his wife served a mission in Fiji. He spoke about the difference between missionary work and athletics: "Only the game is different here. All the boys who have labored here have only one goal, and that is to preach the gospel of Jesus Christ, so something great can be brought into the lives of the people. These young elders are just as devoted to their work here as the young men on the teams of East were in their respective sports."[35]

William McKinley (Mickey) Oswald (1899–1977) was one of the Church's great athletes and teachers. Before his mission, he had earned thirteen (of a

◁ Montage of First Presidency, Council of the Twelve, and Seven Presidents of Seventies, 1924[36]

◁ Evan Stephens (1854–1930) fishing at the pond on his property at 1996 So. State, Salt Lake City, ca. 1925

Considered by many to be the "father of musical progress in the Church," Stephens was the director of the Tabernacle Choir from 1890 to 1914, an indefatigable composer (the current hymnal contains nineteen of his compositions), an instructor of vocal music at L.D.S. University, and the director of music for the YMMIA. Complementing his love for music was his love for nature. "Brother Stephens was an ardent lover of nature; flowers, mountains, streams, rocky peaks and pine clad hills were his side partners. . . . His home on South State Street in Salt Lake City was one of the beauty spots of Zion. With the ornamental trees, shrubs, flowers, weeping willows and a mirror lake filled with trout and enjoyed by water fowl, delighted the eye."[37]

◁ Elder J. Vernon Sharp with an Aymara chief and his wife at Ollantaitomba, Peru, Upper Amazon, South American Mission, June 7, 1927

Elder J. Vernon Sharp wrote in his journal: "June 7. . . . There is a sort of a construction train that leaves twice a week for there [Ollantaitomba] and as to-day is one of those days I decided to go as far as Ollantaitomba as there are said to be some very fine ruins there. . . . While looking over the village we saw some costumed dancers and heard their weird dance music . . . it was the celebration for Pentecost and . . . the Indians from all over had come to celebrate so down we clumb to get in on the fun. . . . No sooner did I enter than I had to take their pictures . . . no sooner was the picture taking done than the chief's wife came up and gave me a handkerchief and upon inquiry found that it meant I was to dance with her. Well I tried to beg off but nothing doing and so we had a nice little dance, much to the enjoyment of all, myself included. Then when that was done all of the damsels came on and before I was thru I had to dance with all which was a total of 12."[38]

△ Elder J. Vernon Sharp (1905–1990) baptizing Carmen Trujillo de Estrada at Santa Ana Falls, South American Mission, ca. 1927[39]

▷ **Downey Girls Chorus in Salt Lake City, ca. 1927**

Front row, left to right: Grace Williams (Porter, director), Elaine Anderson (Armstrong), Mildred Owen (Coffin), and Edna Hendricks (Johnson).

Middle row: Mrs. Frank La Jeneusse, Virgil Burrup (Hartvigsen), Mabel Salvesen, and Dorothy Williams (Palmer).

Back row: Veda Merrill (Hobbs), Lottie Anderson (Almond), Leah Gene Kraemer, Myrtle Merrill (Jorgensen), and Nina Johnson (Almond).

The singers posed prior to their scheduled competitive performance. Virgil Burrup Hartvigsen's (1908–1991) son, Kip, retells their experience: "The group won a regional competition, an accolade which included an invitation to perform in Salt Lake City. All the girls were excited at the prospects of making the big trip to the city, anything but a common occurrence in those days. Once there, Mom remembers the tension of warming up for their part on the all-invitational program. . . . On stage, in the middle of their song, the leg of the piano . . . fell off, the piano crashing to the floor with a multi-toned thunder that echoed through the hall. Mom said in rather understated terms, 'It was difficult for our group to recover after that.'" [40]

▽ **Actors and actresses of the Colonia Dublan Ward, Mexico, 1928**

This is the first drama in the new Dublan chapel.

Left to right: L. Claudeus Bowman, Frank Romney, Hannah S. Call, Zinda Abegg, Alvin Coon, Clessa Moffett, Pamilia Skousen, Joseph Memmott, Velan Call, and Maurine Robinson. [41]

P-1683

△ **Movie star Douglas Fairbanks with Mormon women, October 1927**

This photograph was taken at the time of the Arizona Temple dedication. These women had seen the movie *King of Kings* and had their photograph taken with actor Douglas Fairbanks, who happened to be in the area.

Front row, left to right: Rachael Grant Taylor, Lucy Woodruff Smith (wife of Apostle George Albert Smith), Mary Jack, Elizabeth Snow Ivins, Douglas Fairbanks, Augusta W. Grant, unidentified, unidentified,

unidentified, May Anderson, and Sarah McClelland.

Back row: Addie Howells, unidentified, unidentified, Alice Sheets over Fairbanks's left shoulder, and Leah D. Widstoe

(with black hat and white beads). The two at the end are Martha Smith and Ruth May Fox.[42]

△ **Elder George Wilcken Romney, missionary, British Mission, 1928**

Elder George Romney writes a message for all to read—especially potential converts. Elder Romney would later become the CEO of American Motors, governor of Michigan (1962–1966), and Secretary of Housing and Urban Development (1969–1973) under President Richard M. Nixon.[43]

△ **May Anderson (1864–1946), Primary general president; ca. 1928**

May Anderson was an English convert who emigrated to Utah with her family in 1883. She was actively interested in children's needs and problems throughout her life. Soon after she arrived in Utah, she taught kindergarten in Salt Lake City, and in 1890 she was sustained as general secretary of the Primary. In 1902 she was named the editor of the *Children's Friend.* She held that position until 1940. In 1925 she was called to be the general president of the Primary, and she continued in that position until 1939. May Anderson was crucial in the supervision of the creation and growth of the Primary Children's Hospital, which began as an idea in 1911. She was the first president of its board of trustees, a position she held until 1945.[44]

▷ **Susa Young Gates (1856–1933) and family, four generations, ca. 1932**

Left to right: Susa Young Gates (great-grandmother), Leah Dunford Widstoe (grandmother), Anna Widstoe Wallace (mother), and Joanne Wallace (Koplin).

Susa Young Gates, daughter of Brigham Young and Lucy Bigelow Young, was a productive essayist, novelist, genealogist, teacher, organizer, administrator, Church worker, public speaker, suffragist, and the mother of thirteen children. She was married twice, first to Dr. Alma Dunford (whom she divorced) and then to Jacob Gates. Because of her great influence both inside and outside the Church, she was nicknamed the "thirteenth apostle."

Her son-in-law, John A. Widtsoe, wrote to her in 1899 concerning her accomplishments: "I admire Brother Gates. Without his willingness you could not do so much. So few men are willing to undergo a little personal inconvenience to let their wives do anything. The exceptions are loved so much the more. A man's life is not measured alone by what he accomplishes. More than that, is what he enables others to do."[45]

◁ **Council of Twelve Apostles on the steps of the Salt Lake Temple, April 1931**

Front, left to right: Rudger Clawson, Reed Smoot, George Albert Smith, and George F. Richards.

Middle: Orson F. Whitney, David O. McKay, Joseph Fielding Smith, and James E. Talmage.

Back: Stephen L Richards, Richard R. Lyman, Melvin J. Ballard, and John A. Widtsoe.[46]

◁ **Elder Gordon B. Hinckley and Armand S. Coulam (1914–1984), British Mission, ca. 1935**

In 1961, twenty-six years after his mission, Gordon B. Hinckley was chosen to be an apostle. At that time he stated: "I would like to say that this cause is either true or false. Either this is the kingdom of God, or it is a sham and a delusion. Either Joseph talked with the Father and the Son or he did not. If he did not, we are engaged in a blasphemy. If he did, we have a duty from which none of us can shrink—to declare to the world the living reality of the God of the universe, the Father of us all and his Son the Lord Jesus Christ, the Savior of the world, our Redeemer, the Author of our salvation, the Prince of Peace. I give you my testimony that this is *true*."[47]

▷ **Women canning at the Salt Lake Regional Canning Center, 1936**

In 1900, Joseph F. Smith stated: "You must continue to bear in mind that the temporal and the spiritual are blended. They are not separate. One cannot be carried on without the other. . . . The Latter-day Saints believe not only in the gospel of spiritual salvation, but also in the gospel of temporal salvation."

In April 1936, in the midst of the Great Depression, the Church introduced the Church Security Program (renamed the Church Welfare Program in 1938) to assist the impoverished and unemployed among the Saints. In 1936 President J. Reuben Clark, Jr., asserted: "The real long term objective of the Welfare Plan is the building of character in the members of the Church, givers and receivers, rescuing all that is finest down deep inside of them, and bringing to flower and fruitage the latent richness of the spirit, which after all is the mission and purpose and reason for being of this Church."[48]

◁ Men pose at the food cellar they built under the auspices of the Welfare Program of the East Central Utah Region, April 9, 1938

Lucius Laudie (secretary-treasurer of East Central Utah Security Program) wrote: "All of the work was done on this cellar . . . under the Welfare Plan with Work Slips being issued, for hours contributed, sent to the Bishops of the five Stakes participating, and if any one on the job needed assistance their needs were taken care of by the respective bishops. However, but few who participated called for assistance. Bishops and Ward Leaders, with those in need, all joined hands together in the construction of this cellar."[49]

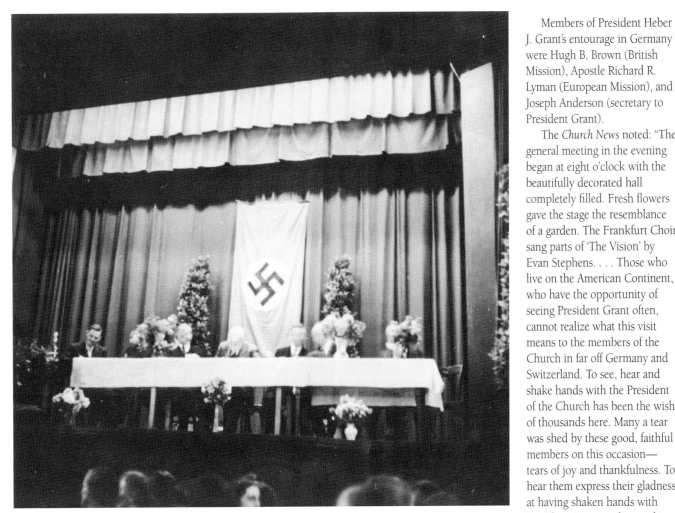

△ President Heber J. Grant and party, Frankfurt Germany, July 1937

In Germany at this time, all public assemblies were required to display the Nazi (National Socialist Party) flag.

Members of President Heber J. Grant's entourage in Germany were Hugh B. Brown (British Mission), Apostle Richard R. Lyman (European Mission), and Joseph Anderson (secretary to President Grant).

The *Church News* noted: "The general meeting in the evening began at eight o'clock with the beautifully decorated hall completely filled. Fresh flowers gave the stage the resemblance of a garden. The Frankfurt Choir sang parts of 'The Vision' by Evan Stephens. . . . Those who live on the American Continent, who have the opportunity of seeing President Grant often, cannot realize what this visit means to the members of the Church in far off Germany and Switzerland. To see, hear and shake hands with the President of the Church has been the wish of thousands here. Many a tear was shed by these good, faithful members on this occasion— tears of joy and thankfulness. To hear them express their gladness at having shaken hands with President Grant, and to see him, though almost eighty-one years of age, reaching his steady hand to each one present, caused us to express our gratitude for a man who so loves the saints in all parts of the world that he gives them the greatest joy of their lives."[50]

▷ **Harold B. Lee and other Salt Lake City officials, 1938**

Left to right: George D. Keyser (commissioner of the Water Department), Ethel McDonald (city recorder), Harold B. Lee (commissioner of the Streets Department), Charles Finlayson (city auditor), William Murdock (commissioner of Public Finance), Pat Goggin (commissioner of Parks), and Mayor E. B. Erwin.

Harold B. Lee was chosen to be on the Salt Lake City Commission when a vacancy was created at the death of Salt Lake City Commissioner Joseph H. Lake in October of 1932. After successfully campaigning in the fall of 1933 for a second term, he visited the First Presidency, writing of the occasion: "Following the election I called on the First Presidency of the Church and had a visit with President A. W. Ivins. I told him it would be my pleasure to counsel with them on any matters in which they were interested. He [told me] that the only counsel he had to offer was that I should take the actions I thought were right. He said, 'I would ten times rather a man . . . make a mistake while doing that which he thought was right than to do right just for policy sake.'"[51]

▷ **Australian Mission basketball team, 1938**

Left to right: Elders John T. Williams, Norman Everett, K. Borton Olsen, Kenneth E. Wright, Frank Bailey, Elder Richardson, and Byron T. Moore.

The *Church News* of July 1938 reported: "A group of Mormon missionaries in Australia have been attracting wide attention among the sport loving people of that country. Recently in Melbourne, the Mormon basketball team was seen in several games against native teams and sports writers frequently commented on the speed and knowledge of the game, declaring the exhibitions to be the best ever seen in Melbourne. Between the halves of one game recently several of the Mormon missionaries gave the audience an exhibition of some of the finer points of American football. They demonstrated, to the delight of the crowd, the spiral pass and dropkick."[52]

◁ Wandamere Ward Sunday School class, Salt Lake City, June 1, 1940[53]

◁ President Heber J. Grant showing blind activist Helen Keller a Braille copy of the Book of Mormon, 1941[54]

△ **Eighty-three-year-old Margaret Fox with extended family, Downey, Idaho, 1942**

Top: Margaret Florenza Green Fox (1859–1951).

Middle row, left to right: Lois Hartvigsen, Bessie Fox Burrup holding Lorre Burrup, Dixie Burrup (at knee), Edward Burrup holding Pamela Keller, and Bonne Hartvigson.

Front row: Gary Dean Henderson, Richard Neil Hartvigson, and Kaye Burrup.

In 1861 Margaret Fox crossed the plains as a two-year-old toddler in the David H. Cannon Company. She was born in Iowa in 1859, the daughter of Nauvoo native Cynthia Ann Mikesell and her husband, British immigrant William Green. At age sixteen, Sister Fox married farmer/sheepherder Thomas James Fox, and they raised their fourteen children in Marsh Valley, Idaho. Widowed in 1905, she supported her youngest children by washing laundry at the Enterprise Hotel of Downey, Idaho. She was also an avid gardener, movie-goer, and Relief Society worker.[55]

△ **Council of the Twelve Apostles, late 1943**

Seated, left to right: Stephen L Richards, Joseph Fielding Smith, George F. Richards, and George Albert Smith.

Standing: Ezra Taft Benson, Spencer W. Kimball, Harold B. Lee, Albert E. Bowen, Charles A. Callis, Joseph F. Merrill, John A. Widtsoe, and Richard R. Lyman.[56]

◁ **Launching of the S.S. *Joseph Smith*, Richmond, California, May 22, 1943**

The Liberty Ship S.S. *Joseph Smith,* named for the Prophet, was activated as a merchant ship for use during World War II. Local Latter-day Saints took part in the launching activities. Oakland Stake President Eugene Hilton spoke about Joseph Smith, and then the Richmond Ward Choir sang two songs. President Hilton's first counselor, W. Glenn Harmon, gave the prayer. Admiral Emory S. Land of the U.S. *Maritime* spoke about Joseph Smith and praised the Church's role in the war effort.[57]

▷ **LDS group serving in the Admiralty Islands, World War II, July 1944**

Seated, left to right: Herbert J. Smith (Hackettstown, N.J., nonmember), Kenneth Austin (Richmond, Ca.), Norman Burr (Los Angeles, Ca.), Ralph Winn (Los Angeles, Ca.), Richard C. Miller (Salt Lake City), Andrew B. Shumway (Preston, Idaho), and Robert Peterson (Salt Lake City).

Standing: John W. Scott (Alexandria, South Dakota, nonmember), Lorin B. Squires (Great Falls, Mont.), E. J. Hawkes (Ogden, Ut.), H. W. Jones (Reno, Nevada, nonmember), Samuel Marsh, Jr. (Minneapolis, Minn., nonmember), and George Shelley (Kingman, Az.).[58]

◁ **Downey Relief Society with "Care Packages" they prepared for family members serving overseas during World War II, 1944**

Fourth from left on the front row is Bessie Fox Burrup, whose package was sent to her son, Clyde, who was serving as a cryptographer in India.[59]

▷ **Branch member with four German prisoners of war who attended the Sunday meetings of the Bradford Branch, Great Britain, ca. 1945; unfortunately all are unidentified**

George F. Poole, a district leader in London, relates his experience with these German prisoners of war: "I had a call from President Brown to visit a prisoner of war camp in England. He had received a letter from a German prisoner of war, and this man had asked for baptism. . . . We went in [the POW camp] and saw this German. . . . I talked to him for a little bit and I felt impressed that we should let him join the Church. So we went to the commandant and asked him if we could baptize [the German]. And so the American said, 'Well, all right, but there's no facilities in the camp.' So I said, 'Well, could we take him outside the camp?' He said, 'All right . . . providing you'll promise that you'll bring him back immediately after you've done this baptism.' . . . And so he was baptized. I confirmed him a member of the Church. . . . [Later] when I was made a counselor in the mission presidency, . . . we walked in through the hall, and I guess there was fifteen or twenty German prisoners of war sitting on the stand. . . . So I said to President Boyer, 'What's those Germans doing on the stand?' . . . He said, 'They're all members of the Church. . . . They've all been converted . . . during the war.' . . . This German who [I baptized] . . . had talked to these other prisoners of war in this camp and had converted all these Germans, and they were wonderful."[60]

PART FIVE

1945

1995

▷ **Prophet and seer, George Albert Smith (1870–1951), ca. 1945**

President George Albert Smith loved the "great out-doors." Along with his many Church responsibilities, he also played a prominent role on the National Council of the Boy Scouts of America, and he was an organizer and president of the Utah Pioneer Trails and Landmarks Association.

A non-Mormon friend of this prophet and seer declared: "He was not a poet or a great financier, nor was he as fine an orator as his father [John Henry Smith], but if ever a man walked the streets of this world who was fit to walk and talk with God, it was George Albert Smith."[1]

◁ **President George Albert Smith and party in Washington, D.C., November 7, 1945**

Left to right: Joseph Anderson (secretary to the First Presidency), Apostle John A. Widtsoe, German S. Ellsworth, President George Albert Smith, Thomas E. McKay (Assistant to the Quorum of Twelve), and Edgar B. Brossard (president of the Washington Stake).

In the background appears the impressive Washington, D.C., LDS chapel. President Smith and the others were in Washington to arrange with U.S. and European government officials for the Church to send food, clothing, and bedding from Church welfare warehouses to needy Church members in Europe. All officials agreed to give 100 percent cooperation. The Church was soon able to supply many of the basic needs for Latter-day Saints in Europe.[2]

▽ **First Presidency, 1947**

Left to right: J. Reuben Clark (1871–1961, first counselor), President George Albert Smith, and David O. McKay (second counselor).[3]

◁ **Rotterdam District missionaries and members loading potatoes and herring for distribution among the Saints in Germany and other areas of war-ravaged Europe, 1947**

In this photo of Rotterdam District missionaries and members, Netherlands Mission president Cornelius Zappey is at left center in a suit and tie. President Zappey worked hard to receive permission from the Dutch government to ship some sixty-six tons of potatoes to the Saints in Germany. Understandably, the Dutch government was initially opposed to this idea.

Despite the affliction caused by the German Nazi regime during World War II, the Dutch Saints showed their love and willingness to sacrifice by donating potatoes to the German members, who were also suffering from the devastation caused by the war. These potatoes were from the Dutch Saints' own Church welfare gardens and had been originally planted for their own use. David O. McKay stated: "This is one of the greatest acts of true Christian conduct. . . . The Dutch Saints are to be congratulated that they can perform this act of welfare service to members of the Church who live in a country which has caused them so much suffering and hardship during recent years."[4]

▷ **President George Albert Smith visiting with pioneer Alma Elizabeth Felt, 1947**

Left to right: President George Albert Smith, Alma Elizabeth Mineer Felt (1855–1950), second counselor David O. McKay, and "Days of '47" queen Calleen Robinson.

Born in Sweden, Alma Mineer (Felt) journeyed west at the age of six in 1861 with the John R. Murdock pioneer company. She remembered entering the Salt Lake Valley: "After three and one-half months of walking over a hot desert, up the rugged hills, and down the hills and canyons, we finally came out of Emigration Canyon, dirty, and ragged. When I saw my mother looking over this valley with the tears streaming down her pale cheeks, she made this remark: 'Is this Zion, and are we at the end of this long, weary journey?' Of course to me as a child, this had been a delightful pleasure jaunt, and I remember it as only fun."

She married Joseph Henry Felt in 1875, and they became the parents of six children; they adopted four more children.[5]

△ **Stake presidents working on a welfare farm, Utah County, July 1948**

Left to right: Presidents J. Earl Lewis (West Utah Stake), Victor J. Bird (Utah Stake), Charles E. Rowan (Provo Stake), and Golden L. Woolf (East Provo Stake).[6]

▷ **First Presidency, ca. 1951**

Left to right: Stephen L Richards (first counselor), President David O. McKay, and J. Reuben Clark (second counselor).[7]

◁ **U.S. Secretary of Agriculture Ezra Taft Benson and his assistant Arthur Haycock, ca. 1953**

Apostle Ezra Taft Benson served as President Dwight D. Eisenhower's Secretary of Agriculture for eight years, beginning in 1953. A Washington reporter noticed the difference between Elder Benson and the usual Washington politician: "[He] acts like a man whose conscience is always clear—his testimony [before Senate committees] will be the same next week or the week after or a year from now. He doesn't have to remember what he said to an opposition senator at the last meeting. This is a built-in ulcer-saving device, not always found in Washington."[8]

▷ **Apostle Joseph Fielding Smith in the cockpit of a fighter jet, 1954**

Left to right: Colonel Alma G. Winn, Elder Joseph Fielding Smith, and General Maxwell E. Rich.

Joseph Fielding Smith was born in 1876 in pioneer Salt Lake City. To put that date in perspective, it is the same year Col. Custer's 7th Cavalry forces were wiped out in the Battle of the Little Big Horn. As well as being an apostle since 1910, Elder Smith served for nearly sixty-four years as assistant Church Historian and then Church Historian. But his interests were not just for things of the past; he was also curious about all facets of modern life. One of these facets was flying, and his attention was especially drawn to military jets. On June 9, 1954, he took his first flight in a fighter: "Colonel Alma Winn invited me to take a ride with him in a jet plane. . . . It was a wonderful experience to travel in such a plane at about 500 miles per hour." Five months later he flew with Colonel Winn again: "We pierced the dark heavy clouds up into the clear sunshine. It was the most beautiful scene I can remember, as the tops of the highest peaks penetrated the clouds like islands. The clouds on top were perfectly white [and those] below extremely dark, with some rain falling later."[9]

▷ **Apostle Harold B. Lee in front of chapel, 8069th Army Unit Replacement Zone, Pusan, Korea, September 1954**

Left to right: Captain Johnson (chaplain of the 8069th Army Unit), President Hilton A. Robertson (Japanese Mission), Brigadier General Richard S. Whitcomb (commanding general of the Pusan military post), Elder Harold B. Lee, Lieutenant Colonel Darkey (chief of chaplains, Pusan), 1st Lieutenant Parmor (chaplain), and Lieutenant Colonel Merriel.

Harold B. Lee recorded the following about his 1954 tour: "We met with a total 1,563 Latter-day Saint boys in military service, in our conferences in Japan, Korea, Okinawa, the Philippines, and Guam. . . . In every camp where we went, under military orders, we were accorded every privilege that could be accorded one going into those areas, and the first procedure was invariably an introduction to the commanding general. . . . They know our boys. They know of the work of the Latter-day Saints. . . . Their attitude towards our boys is best summed up in what General Richard S. Whitcomb said. . . . 'I have always known the members of your Church to be a substantial people. Here in the Pusan area I have the largest court-martial responsibility of any command, . . . but I never have had one of your faith brought before me for a court martial or disciplinary action.'"[10]

◁ **Swiss Temple, Zollikofen, Switzerland, ca. 1955**

The Swiss Temple was the first European temple. It was dedicated on September 11, 1955, by David O. McKay.[11]

△ **Golden Wedding Anniversary, Ed and Bessie Burrup, both age seventy-two, 1957**

Brother Ed Burrup had just recovered from a heart attack when this photograph was taken. He died in 1963. Bessie died in 1982 at the age of ninety-seven. They are buried side by side in Downey, Idaho.[12]

▷ **Giving the "sacrament gem" scripture for Sunday School opening exercises, Boise Ninth Ward, Boise, Idaho, 1958**

Left to right: Harold Howells, Jr., Loraine Brady, L. D. Holsinger, Wallace D. Plant, and Wallace Houck, at the stand.[13]

△ **Missionary crossing the English Channel, 1958**

Carl W. Olson, at right, a missionary serving in the Swedish Mission, is sleeping in a deck chair aboard a ship en route to the dedication of the London Temple.[14]

▷ **Belle Spafford speaking at the annual general Relief Society conference, October 1959**

Marion Isabelle Sims Smith Spafford (1895–1982) was the president of the Relief Society from 1945 to 1974. She also served two terms (1968–1970) as president of the National Council of Women. As president of the Relief Society, she placed special importance on strengthening the family and the community. President Spafford was married to Earl Spafford, and they were the parents of two children. In 1976 she listed what she had learned in eighty-one years of life: "That life is very short. That time is extremely valuable and should not be dissipated. That the teachings of the Church are sound and reasonable. Obedience to them brings sure rewards. Disobedience brings naught but sorrow. That the body is a fine precision instrument designed for accomplishment. It is folly . . . to neglect or abuse it. That adversity is the common lot of everyone. . . . That family ties are sacred. No effort is too great to safeguard them. That friends are the savor that brings flavor and sweet refreshment to life. That liberty is a priceless heritage. It should not be allowed to perish from this earth. These things I know of a certainty."[15]

△ **Elder Ronald G. Watt on the "Iron Horse," Coventry, British Mission, 1960**

Elder Ronald Watt wrote: "When I first arrived in the British Mission in July 1959, I was sent to Swansea in South Wales. I bought a bicycle which I described as my 'Iron Horse.' It was a heavy, old bike that had seen better days. I rode that bike all over the hills of South Wales. After six months I purchased a newer, lighter bike. It was a relief to get rid of my heavy one, but for some reason instead of selling it I left it in the shed. Not long after that I was going down a hill when I was forced to jam on both the front and back brakes to avoid hitting a car. The wheels froze, and I found myself on the ground. The front wheel of the bicycle was doubled up. I rode 'Iron Horse' again until I got a new wheel. About a month later while riding my lightweight bicycle a car made a right hand turn in front of me, demolishing my bike. . . . I went back to my old 'Iron Horse.' I never bought another bicycle after that. I was later transferred to Coventry and the old bike went with me. It faithfully performed its job the rest of my mission and never got a scratch on it." [16]

▽ **Aaronic Priesthood, Loughborough Branch, Leicester Stake, Great Britain, April 1961**

Front: Ray Eaton.

Back, left to right: David Murray, Malcomb Hayes, Terry Bryan, Arthur Bailey, John Simpson, John Tyler, and Charles Eaton.[18]

△ **Christmas at the home of Harold and Dorothy Allsop, Downey, Idaho, 1960**

Children, left to right: Jay Burrup (neighbor), Cory Allsop, and Brynne Allsop (Heaton).

Adults: Dorothy and Harold Allsop.

Harry Allsop served the rural southeast Idaho community as pharmacist and drugstore owner, ward Scoutmaster, bishopric member, and school board member. Dorothy helped run the drugstore and dedicated her life to Church and community service and to rearing their four children, Brynne (Heaton), Cory, Kimberly (Johnson), and Kristen (Bearnson).[17]

▷ **President John F. Kennedy giving a speech in the Salt Lake Tabernacle, September 26, 1963**

Left to right: President David O. McKay, Senator Frank Moss, and U.S. President John Fitzgerald Kennedy.

Upon meeting the Chief Executive, President David O. McKay greeted him with "Hello, Mr. President!" John F. Kennedy replied, "Hello, Mr. President!" In the Tabernacle, President Kennedy gave an hour-and-a-half talk mostly concerned with foreign policy. He concluded his speech by stating the importance of diplomacy to "support the world of freedom. For as we discharge that commitment, we are heeding the command which Brigham Young heard from the Lord more than a century ago—the command he conveyed to his followers: 'Go as pioneers . . . to a land of peace.'"[19]

◁ **President David O. McKay with his beloved wife, Emma Ray Riggs, Huntsville, Utah**

The love shared between President David O. McKay and his wife, Emma Ray, was world renowned. In a letter written on the occasion of their twentieth wedding anniversary, Apostle McKay expressed his feelings: "*January second Nineteen One* marked the beginning of a new year, the beginning of a new century, the beginning of a new and happy Life! I loved you that morning with the love and fire of youth. It was pure and sincere. You were my heart's treasure, no bride more sweet, and pure, and beautiful! But this morning . . . I think I didn't know what love was when I took you as my bride. It was but as the light of a star compared with [the] glorious sunlight of Love that fills my soul to-day."[20]

△ **Elsie Clegg (1890–1969) with her handiwork, 1964**

Elsie Clegg was born in Marsh Valley, Idaho, shortly before Idaho was granted statehood in 1890. In 1907 she married Joseph Clegg, and they became the parents of one daughter, Donna Clegg (Evans). Unfortunately, Joseph died from cancer in 1933 during the depression. Elsie never remarried, supporting herself and her daughter variously as a telephone operator, seamstress, and hotel maid. She brought in additional income with her abilities for the custom designing and stitching of quilts, pillowcases, and bedding. She learned her award-winning handiwork from her mother, Hannah Maria Burrup, who was the Grant Ward (Idaho) Relief Society president for twenty years. Her mother must have been a good teacher, for Elsie's sisters, Lula Anderson, Zina Barnes, and Vivian Symons, also excelled in this handiwork.[21]

▽ **Family home evening, Guatemala, 1969**

Miguel Batz and his family holding family home evening. Elder Batz was a farmer in the mountains of Totonicapan and a leader in the local branch.[22]

◁ **President Joseph Fielding Smith, prophet and seer, reading with a young friend, bridging the generations, ca. 1970**

One of President Joseph Fielding Smith's grandsons remembered: "President Smith liked pie and he liked children; he liked good books, and he loved to hear Jessie [Jessie Evans Smith, his wife] sing. . . . Though Joseph Fielding Smith served as an apostle for more than sixty-two years, he constantly taught his family that the blessings of the kingdom of heaven were not associated with office or position. His doctrine was that true greatness is found only in the family."[23]

▷ **The First Presidency, 1972**

Left to right: N. Eldon Tanner, President Harold B. Lee, and Marion G. Romney.

After being sustained as prophet and president on October 6, 1972, Harold B. Lee spoke of his deepest feelings: "I am moved with emotions beyond expression as I have felt the true love and bonds of brotherhood. There has been here an overwhelming spiritual endowment, attesting, no doubt, that in all likelihood we are in the presence of personages, seen and unseen, who are in attendance. Who knows but that even our Lord and Master would be near us on such an occasion as this, for we, and the world, must never forget that this is his Church, and under his almighty direction we are to serve!"[24]

▷ **President Spencer W. Kimball being honored at the Fiji Area conference, Suva, Fiji, February, 1976**

Seated, left to right: Sarah M. Tanner, N. Eldon Tanner, unidentified, President Spencer Kimball, and Camilla E. Kimball.

In early 1976, although burdened with influenza for part of the tour, President Kimball presided over nine area conferences in three weeks in America Samoa, Western Samoa, New Zealand, Fiji, Tonga, Australia, and Tahiti. To the Saints of Fiji he stated: "This is another of a series of area conferences, the first of which was held in Manchester, England, in 1971. . . . These inspiring meetings have made it possible for the leaders of the Church to become acquainted on a personal basis with leaders and members of the Church residing throughout the world. They also dramatize . . . the truly international character of the Church. . . . Earlier this evening a beautiful program was held in this room by the people of this community. . . . We extend to each and every one of them our heartfelt thanks and appreciation."[25]

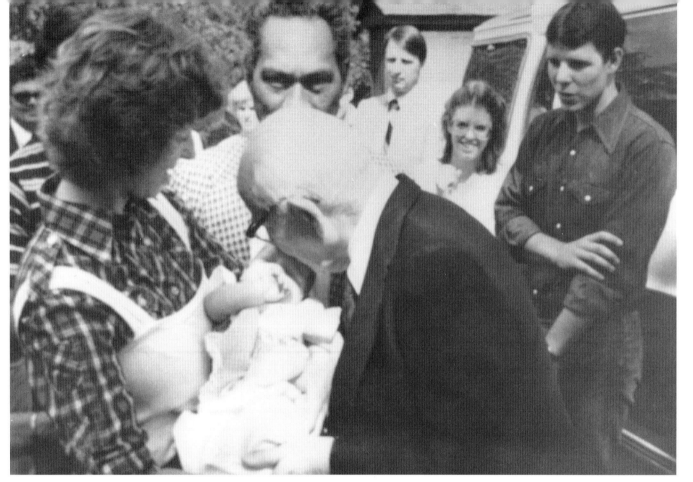

▽ **Maria Grazia Musso Bocca playing "cut the flour," Turin, Italy, 1977**

Sister Maria Bocca after playing one of the American elders' favorite home evening games, "cut the flour": flour is packed in a cup and emptied onto a plate. Then a coin is placed on the flour. The players take turns carefully cutting away sections of flour. The unlucky player who collapses the flour must push the coin off the plate with his or her nose before sneezing.

Maria Bocca and her eight-year-old son, Alberto, were baptized on the same day in 1968, just two years after Ezra Taft Benson rededicated Italy for missionary work. She and her two children have been stalwarts of the Church in Northern Italy. The Bocca home, an attic apartment in central Turin, has been a hospitable retreat for missionaries in the Milan Mission.[27]

△ **President Spencer W. Kimball taking time for members, kissing a baby**

President Spencer W. Kimball's spirit is well illustrated by this story told by Dr. Norman Vincent Peale: "[There was] a woman who was in O'Hare Airport in Chicago during a big snowstorm. . . . Thousands of people were stranded. Her money had run out, she had a two-year-old child, and the child was hungry and dirty. The woman was . . . pregnant and had been told not to hold this child because it might have an adverse effect on her physically. So the child was on the floor. . . . The woman was in one line after another trying to buy a ticket to a Michigan point. People were criticizing her because she would reach forward with her foot to push the child up in the line as the line moved along, because she couldn't pick the child up. She was in anguish when a man approached her with a kindly smile on his face. He said, 'Young lady, it appears to me that you need help.' He took the dirty, little two-year-old child in his arms and loved it, patted it on the back. . . . Then he went to the people in the line and he told them about the woman—how she had to get a flight out to Michigan. They agreed, under the influence of his spirit, to let her go ahead of them. He took her to the flight and got her started on her way. . . . Now that's a simple story, but how many people would do it? Jesus would do it, and a representative of Jesus on earth did do it."[26]

◁ **Freetown-Wellington Branch Presidency, ca. 1988**

Left to right: John Sivalie, first counselor; Michael Samura, president; Theophilus Cole, second counselor; Samuel Brown, clerk.

On June 8, 1978, the First Presidency announced: "We have pleaded long and earnestly . . . spending many hours in the Upper Room of the Temple supplicating the Lord for divine guidance.

"He has heard our prayers, and by revelation has confirmed that the long-promised day has come when every faithful, worthy man in the Church may receive the holy priesthood, with power to exercise its divine authority, and enjoy with his loved ones every blessing that flows therefrom, including the blessings of the temple. Accordingly, all worthy male members of the Church may be ordained to the priesthood without regard for race or color." This revelation was unanimously sustained at the 148th semiannual general conference on September 30, 1978.[28]

◁ **U.S. President Ronald Reagan visiting the Ogden Area Welfare Service Center cannery, September 10, 1982**

President Ronald Reagan toured the Ogden, Utah, welfare facility to see for himself an example of a volunteer welfare program. Among the volunteers that day were several homemakers, a dentist, a doctor, welfare recipients, an IRS administrator, and a mechanic. President Reagan stated: "Here is an entire industry. . . . It is manned by volunteers, people from the Church. The foodstuffs that are here are raised by volunteers, picked by volunteers. They're brought here. They're canned. . . . And they're used to distribute to those people who have real need here in the state of Utah and all over the country, for that matter. . . . It's an idea that once characterized our nation. It's an idea that should be reborn nationwide."[29]

△ **Missionaries in the California San Jose Mission, October 1983**

As Church missionaries were being allowed into more and more foreign countries, the Church also proselyted non–English-speaking people in the United States.

Left to right: Elders Steven H. Moore (Vietnamese language), Randy Barney (Thai), Brian A. Coleman (Vietnamese), Scott R. Christensen (standing behind, English), and Yotin Tanomrat (Thai, from Thailand).[30]

▷ **President Gordon B. Hinckley and his wife, Marjorie Pay Hinckley, at the dedication of the Mexico City Temple, December 1983**[31]

▷ **The First Presidency, October 1989**

Left to right: Gordon B. Hinckley, President Ezra Taft Benson, and Thomas S. Monson.[32]

△ **Freiberg Germany Temple, 1991**

The Freiberg Germany Temple was dedicated on June 29 and 30, 1985, by President Gordon B. Hinckley. It was the first and only temple built in a communist bloc nation. About this sacred House of God President Hinckley stated: "The faithful Saints sacrificed their money, their jewelry, their comfort to assist in building that temple. One of their number who attended the dedication wrote: 'There was a solemn stillness, and there was not a dry eye. The sun was shining after a long time. . . . You could sense gladness and enthusiasm and the wish for a never-ending harmony. . . . Tears, laughter, and gladness; everything was present.'"[33]

△ **Book of Mormon project, Monrovia, 1988**

Concerning the dedication and opening of Africa for the preaching of the gospel, Elder Alexander B. Morrison of the First Quorum of the Seventy stated: "I believe the Lord has had the people of Africa in preparation for this day. They have great dignity, and a strong eagerness to learn. They are ready for the truth, and, when they hear it, they recognize and accept it."[34]

△ **Primary, Freetown-Goderich Branch, Sierra Leone, West Africa, August 1988**

Front row, left to right: Branch President Christian George with the Primary children (all unidentified).

Back row: Iliene Fisher, Mary Jackson, and Adriana Orleans.[35]

▽ **Elder Jon Trent Warner in Bulgaria, 1990**

Elder Jon Trent Warner was a missionary in the Austria East Mission. He, along with other elders, received a change in assignment in late 1990 and became among the first missionaries since 1900 to proselytize in Bulgaria. The summer before, in 1989, as Mikhail Gorbachev's "glasnost" began stirring change in the long-locked communist bloc nations of Europe, missionary work had tentatively proceeded in Russia. By the summer of 1990, there were five hundred members in the Leningrad Branch, which had been organized on December 3, 1989. As repression fell, the Church began to "take hold" among the people in these nations.

Elder Jon Trent Warner is a direct-line descendant of Native American Shoshone Chief Sagwitch, who led his northern Utah band of more than three hundred people into the Church in May 1873.[36]

▷ **The Mormon Tabernacle Choir, St. Basil's on Red Square, Moscow, Russia, June 24, 1991**

In June of 1990 it was announced that for the first time in history, the Tabernacle Choir would tour Moscow and Leningrad as well as nine other European cities. The tour would take place in June 1991. The choir performed in the famous Bolshoi Theater in Moscow and in Leningrad [St. Petersburg] and recorded songs to be broadcast later. At a dinner following the choir's June 24 Moscow performance, it was announced that Russia had given official recognition to The Church of Jesus Christ of Latter-day Saints.

The tour also included cities in Germany, France, Switzerland, Hungary, Austria, Czechoslovakia, and Poland.[37]

◁ President Howard W. Hunter (1907–1995), prophet and seer[38]

▷ President Gordon B.
Hinckley, prophet and seer[39]

Notes

Part One: *1820–1846*

1. Joseph Smith, *History of the Church of Jesus Christ of Latter-day Saints,* ed. Brigham H. Roberts, 7 vols. (Salt Lake City: Deseret Book Company, 1978), 1:4–6. Photograph courtesy Historical Department, Archives Division, The Church of Jesus Christ of Latter-day Saints, Salt Lake City, Utah (hereafter LDS Church Archives). Photographer: George E. Anderson, 1907.

2. Joseph Smith–History 1:34. Oliver Cowdery, "Letter VIII," *Times and Seasons* vol. 2, no. 13 (May 1, 1941):391. Photograph courtesy LDS Church Archives. George E. Anderson, 1907.

3. Joseph Smith–History 1:57–58. Illustration courtesy Utah State Historical Society. Photograph of an oil painting owned by the Reorganized Church of Jesus Christ of Latter Day Saints.

4. "Oliver Cowdery to W. W. Phelps," *Messenger and Advocate* (October 1834), 14. Photograph courtesy LDS Church Archives. Charles W. Carter Collection, n.d.

5. D&C 135:3. Photograph courtesy LDS Church Archives. A Charles W. Carter photograph of a daguerreotype of an oil painting of Joseph Smith owned by the Reorganized Church of Jesus Christ of Latter Day Saints.

6. David Whitmer, *An Address to All Believers in Christ: by a Witness to the Divine Authenticity of The Book of Mormon* (Richmond Missouri: David Whitmer, 1887), 8. Illustration courtesy LDS Historical Department. Engraved by H. B. Hall and Sons, 1883.

7. *History of the Church,* 1:39–41. Photograph courtesy LDS Church Archives. George E. Anderson, 1907.

8. *History of the Church,* 1:74–78. Illustration courtesy Utah State Historical Society.

9. Parley P. Pratt, *Autobiography of Parley Parker Pratt,* 3rd ed. (Salt Lake City: Deseret Book Company, 1938), 37. Photograph of daguerreotype courtesy LDS Church Archives. Marsena Cannon, ca. 1853.

10. Parley P. Pratt, *Mormonism Unveiled: Zion's Watchman Unmasked* (New York: O. Pratt and E. Fordham, 1838), 40–41. Photograph courtesy LDS Church Archives. A Fox and Symons copy of an original, n.d.

11. *History of Geauga and Lake Counties, Ohio* (Philadelphia: Williams Brothers, 1878), 248. Photograph courtesy LDS Archives. Samuel T. Whitaker, ca. 1900.

12. *History of the Church,* 1:261–65. Photograph courtesy LDS Church Archives. Unknown, ca. 1900.

13. Orson F. Whitney, *Life of Heber C. Kimball,* 2nd ed. (Salt Lake City: Stevens and Wallis, 1945), 298–99. Photograph of daguerreotype courtesy LDS Church Archives. Marsena Cannon, ca. 1853.

14. D&C 109:5. Nancy Naomi Alexander Tracy, *The Diary of Nancy Naomi Alexander Tracy* (Florence Tracy Hall, 1956), 11. Photograph courtesy LDS Church Archives. George E. Anderson, 1907.

15. Dean Jessee, ed., *The Papers of Joseph Smith: Volume 1, Autobiographical and Historical Writings* (Salt Lake City: Deseret Book Company, 1989), 168. Etching from frontispiece of J. H. Kennedy, *Early Days of Mormonism* (New York: Charles Scribner's Sons, 1888).

16. *History of the Church,* 7:435. Photograph courtesy LDS Church Archives. Savage and Ottinger, n.d.

17. *History of the Church,* 1:390–91. Illustration courtesy LDS Church Archives. Engraved by Charles B. Hall, n.d.

18. *History of the Church,* 3:190–91. Illustration courtesy LDS Church Archives. Engraved by Charles B. Hall, n.d.

19. *Times and Seasons,* December 1, 1840, 236. Alvah Boggs, "Testimony, 1956," typescript on microfilm, LDS Church Archives. Image courtesy LDS Church Archives.

20. Margaret Mann Foutz, "Haun's Mill Massacre", holograph [n.d.], LDS Church Archives. Etching from T.B.H. Stenhouse, *The Rocky Mountain Saints* (New York: D. Appleton and Company, 1873), 97.

21. D&C 121:1–3. Photograph courtesy LDS Archives. J. T. Hicks, ca. 1878.

22. *History of the Church,* 3:375. *Times and Seasons* (October 1, 1842), 936–37. Illustration original credit: "Aus d. Kunstanst d. Bibl. Instit. in Hildbhsn [trans.: From the Art Institution of the Biblical Institute of Hildburhausen], n.d.

23. Photograph of daguerreotype courtesy LDS Church Archives. Probably taken by Lucian Foster, ca. 1846.

24. Orson Hyde, *A Voice from Jerusalem* (Liverpool: P. P. Pratt, 1842), 29. Photograph of daguerreotype courtesy LDS Church Archives. Marsena Cannon, ca. 1853.

25. *Messenger and Advocate* (August 1836), 357. *History of the Church,* 6:401–2. Illustration courtesy Utah State Historical Society.

26. *Diary of Nancy Tracy,* 20–21. Photograph courtesy LDS Church Archives. Brigham H. Roberts, ca. 1885.

27. Photograph of tintype courtesy LDS Church Archives. Unknown, n.d.

28. As quoted in Carol Cornwall Madsen, *In Their Own Words: Women and the Story of Nauvoo* (Salt Lake City: Deseret Book Company, 1994), 180. Photograph of daguerreotype courtesy LDS Church Archives. Possibly Lucian Foster, ca. 1845–1846.

29. *History of the Church,* 6:621–22. Photograph courtesy LDS Church Archives. B. H. Roberts, ca. 1885.

30. Lucy Mack Smith, *History of Joseph Smith* (Salt Lake City: Bookcraft, 1958), 324–25. Illustration courtesy Utah State Historical Society. Engraved by Charles B. Hall, n.d.

31. Vilate M. Kimball to Heber C. Kimball, June 30, 1844. Photocopy of holograph, LDS Church Archives. Illustration courtesy Utah State Historical Society. Engraved by H. B. Halls and Sons, ca. 1888.

32. *History of the Church,* 7:231–32. Photograph of daguerreotype courtesy LDS Church Archives. Lucian Foster, ca. 1845.

33. "Lines, Written on the Birth of an Infant Son of Mrs. Emma, widow of the Late General Joseph Smith," *Times and Seasons* 5 (December 1, 1844):735. Photograph courtesy Utah State Historical Society. Unknown, ca. 1845.

34. Willard Richards Journal, LDS Archives. Also quoted in Richard Holzapfel and T. Jeffery Cottle, *Old Mormon Nauvoo 1839–1846: Historic Photographs and Guide* (Provo, Utah: Grandin Book Company, 1990), 75–76. Photograph of daguerreotype courtesy LDS Church Archives. Lucian Foster, 1845.

35. "Diary of Lorenzo Dow Young," *Utah Historical Quarterly* (1946), 14:133; diary entry for February 1, 1846. Illustration courtesy LDS Church Archives. Engraved by Charles B. Hall, n.d..

36. Oscar Osburn Winther, ed., *A friend of the Mormons: the Private Papers and Diary of Thomas Leiper Kane* (San Francisco: Gelber-Lilienthal, 1937), 17–18. Illustration courtesy Utah State Historical Society. Etched by Frederick Piercy, ca. 1853.

Part Two: *1847–1877*

1. "Letter II," *New York Herald,* April 8, 1852. Also quoted in Leonard J. Arrington, *Brigham Young: American Moses* (New York: Alfred A. Knopf, 1985), 409. Photograph of daguerreotype courtesy LDS Church Archives. Marsena Cannon, ca. 1850.

2. William Clayton journal as quoted in *An Intimate Chronicle: The Journals of William Clayton,* edited by George D. Smith (Salt Lake City: Signature Books, 1991), 300. Illustration courtesy LDS Church Archives. Engraved by Charles B. Hall, n.d.

3. *An Intimate Chronicle,* 319. Illustration courtesy LDS Church Archives. Engraved by Frederick Piercy, ca. 1853.

4. Sophia Lois Goodridge (Hardy) Diary, Typescript, Utah State Historical Society. Can also be found in Kenneth L. Holmes, editor, *Covered Wagon Women: Diaries and Letters from the Western Trails, 1840–1890* (Glendale, Calif.: The Arthur H. Clark Company, 1983), 2:218–19. Illustration courtesy LDS Church Archives. Engraved by Frederick Piercy, ca. 1853.

5. As quoted in Susan Arrington Madsen, *I Walked to Zion: True Stories of Young Pioneers on the Mormon Trail* (Salt Lake City: Deseret Book Company, 1994), 112. Photograph courtesy Utah State Historical Society. Charles R. Savage, 1866.

6. Photograph courtesy LDS Church Archives. Charles R. Savage, 1866.

7. Photograph courtesy LDS Church Archives. Charles R. Savage, 1866.

8. As quoted in *Covered Wagon Women,* 3:273. Photograph courtesy private possession. Unknown, ca. 1857.

9. Photograph courtesy LDS Church Archives. Charles W. Carter, ca. 1867.

10. Photograph courtesy LDS Church Archives. Charles W. Carter, ca. 1867.

11. Photograph courtesy LDS Church Archives. Unknown, n.d.

12. Wilford Woodruff Journals, July 24, 1847, microfilm of holograph. Illustration courtesy LDS Church Archives. Engraved by Charles B. Hall.

13. Robert Pixton Reminiscence [n.d.], p. 25, photocopy of holograph courtesy Sheri E. Slaughter. Photograph courtesy LDS Church Archives. Edward Martin, ca. 1866.

14. Andrew Jenson, *Church Chronology,* 2nd ed. (Salt Lake City: Deseret News, 1899), 34. Photograph courtesy LDS Church Archives. R. D. Adams, n.d.

15. Illustration courtesy LDS Church Archives. Originally etched by H. B. Hall and Sons, ca. 1883

16. Julina Markham Crow, "History of the Life of Stephen Markham," 22, typescript, LDS Church Archives. Photograph courtesy LDS Church Archives. James H. Crockwell, 1893.

17. Wilford Woodruff Journals, February 14, 1853, microfilm of holograph, LDS Church Archives. Photograph of daguerreotype courtesy LDS Church Archives. Marsena Cannon, February 14, 1853.

18. Jules Remy, *A Journey to Great-Salt-Lake City,* 2 vols. (London: W. Jeffs, 1861), 1:190–93. Engraving courtesy LDS Church Archives. Engraved by Frederick Piercy, 1853.

19. Engraving courtesy Utah State Historical Society. Engraved by Frederick Piercy, 1853.

20. Sabin Family History [ca. 1963], Photocopy of typescript, LDS Church Archives. Photograph of daguerreotype courtesy LDS Church Archives. Unknown, 1851.

21. Photograph of daguerreotype courtesy LDS Church Archives. Marsena Cannon, ca. 1853.

22. As quoted in Janet Roberts Balmforth, "Biography of Robert David Roberts" [n.d.], typescript copy courtesy John Balmforth. Mary Branigan Crandall, "Autobiography of a Noble Woman," *Young Woman's Journal,* vol. 6, no. 9 (June 1895), 428. Etching from Mrs. T.B.H. Stenhouse, *Tell It All* (Hartford, Conn.: A. D. Worthington and Co., 1874), 225.

23. Photograph of ambrotype courtesy LDS Church Archives. Photographer unknown, 1855.

24. Photograph of ambrotype courtesy LDS Church Archives. Unknown, ca. 1857.

25. Photograph courtesy LDS Church Archives. Unknown, ca. 1870.

26. Emmeline B. Wells, "Biography of Mary Ann Angell Young," *Juvenile Instructor,* February 26, 1891, 95. Photograph of daguerreotype courtesy LDS Church Archives. Marsena Cannon, ca. 1853.

27. Mark Twain, *Roughing It* (Hartford, Conn.: American Publishing Company, 1872), 112–13. Photograph courtesy University of Utah, Special Collections. From an ambrotype. Unknown, ca. 1857.

28. Photograph of daguerreotype courtesy LDS Church Archives. Unknown, ca. 1859.

29. Photograph of ambrotype courtesy LDS Church Archives. Unknown, 1858.

30. George A. and Bathsheba Smith to John H. and Sarah Martin, January 4, 1864, Historian's Office Letterpress copybooks, microfilm, LDS Church Archives. Photograph courtesy Utah State Historical Society. David A. Burr, 1858.

31. Joseph C. Rich Journal, microfilm of holograph, Joseph Coulson Rich Collection, LDS Church Archives. Photograph courtesy LDS Church Archives. Unknown, 1860

32. Joseph C. Rich to Ann Eliza Hunter, November 1, 1868, microfilm of holograph, Joseph Coulson Rich Collection, LDS Church Archives. Photograph courtesy LDS Church Archives. Unknown, ca. 1860.

33. Photograph courtesy LDS Church Archives. Charles W. Carter, n.d.

34. Photograph of ambrotype courtesy LDS Church Archives. Unknown, ca. 1864.

35. Richard F. Burton, *The City of the Saints and Across the Rocky Mountains to California,* edited by Fawn M. Brodie (New York: Alfred A. Knopf, 1963), 503–4. Photograph courtesy LDS Church Archives. Unknown, n.d.

36. As quoted in William Mulder and A. Russell Mortensen, eds., *Among the Mormons* (Lincoln: University of Nebraska Press, 1973), 335–36. Photograph courtesy LDS Church Archives. Charles W. Carter, 1863.

37. Photograph courtesy LDS Church Archives. Charles R. Savage, 1863.

38. Journal History of the Church, March 4, 1865, p. 1, LDS Church Archives. Photograph courtesy LDS Church Archives. Savage and Ottinger, 1865.

39. Richard F. Burton, *The City of the Saints,* 263–65. Photograph courtesy LDS Historical Department. Charles R. Savage, ca. 1864.

40. *Deseret Evening News* (July 22, 1911), 26. Photograph courtesy Utah State Historical Society. Unknown, 1865.

41. Mary Bradshaw Richards, *Camping Out in the Yellowstone, 1882,* edited by William W. Slaughter (Salt Lake City: University of Utah Press, 1994), 7–8. Photograph courtesy LDS Church Archives. Charles R. Savage, ca. 1866.

42. William Clayton, "Come, Come, Ye Saints," *Hymns of The Church of Jesus Christ of Latter-day Saints* (Salt Lake City: The Church of Jesus Christ of Latter-day Saints, 1985), 30. Photograph courtesy LDS Church Archives. Unknown, ca. 1866.

43. Identification per George Shelley, *Early History of American Fork* (American Fork, Utah, 1945), 89. Photograph courtesy LDS Church Archives. Unknown, ca. 1866.

44. Eliza R. Snow, *Biography and Family Record of Lorenzo Snow* (Salt Lake City: Deseret News Company, 1884), 407–9, 421. Photograph courtesy LDS Church Archives. Charles W. Carter, 1867.

45. Photograph courtesy Utah State Historical Society. Charles R. Savage, n.d.

46. Manuscript History, July 21–23, 1868, Pinto Ward, Saint George Stake, LDS Church Archives. Photograph courtesy Utah State Historical Society. Unknown, 1868.

47. Andrew Love Neff, *History of Utah* (Salt Lake City: Deseret News Press, 1940), 398–409. Photograph courtesy Utah State Historical Society. Savage and Ottinger, 1866.

48. Photograph courtesy Utah State Historical Society. Possibly Charles R. Savage, 1869.

49. Photograph courtesy LDS Church Archives. Unknown, 1869.

50. Photograph courtesy LDS Church Archives. Charles W. Carter, 1869.

51. Photograph courtesy Utah State Historical Society. Andrew J. Russell, 1869.

52. Photograph courtesy LDS Church Archives. Charles W. Carter, 1870.

53. Michael Bennett Leavitt, *Fifty Years in Theatrical Management* (New York: Broadway Publishing Company, 1912), 404, 409. Photograph courtesy LDS Church Archives. Unknown, 1870.

54. "An Exemplary Indian," *Deseret News Weekly,* 33 (May 7, 1884): 246. Photograph courtesy LDS Church Archives. Charles W. Carter, n.d.

55. Photograph courtesy Utah State Historical Society. Unknown, 1866.

56. As quoted in Merlo J. Pusey, *Builders of the Kingdom* (Provo, Utah: Brigham Young University Press, 1981), 209. Photograph courtesy University of Utah Special Collections. Charles R. Savage, 1874.

57. Compiled C. R. Savage Material, compiled by Emma Jane Savage Jensen, 1940, microfilm of typescript, LDS Church Archives. Photograph courtesy Utah State Historical Society. Charles R. Savage, 1870.

58. As quoted in William G. Hartley, "Samuel D. Chambers," *New Era* 4 (June 1974): 48–49. Photograph courtesy LDS Church Archives. Unknown, ca. 1908.

59. Photograph courtesy LDS Church Archives. Jesse A. Tye, 1875.

60. *Millennial Star,* 37 (July 5, 1875): 426–27. Photograph courtesy Utah State Historical Society. Unknown, n.d.

61. *Deseret News* 24 (April 28, 1875): 194. Photograph courtesy LDS Church Archives. Charles R. Savage, 1875.

62. William Dobbie Kuhre, "Recollections of temple quarry, Little Cottonwood Canyon, and Old Granite City" [n.d.], pp. 5–6, photocopy of typescript, LDS Church Archives. Photograph courtesy LDS Church Archives. Charles W. Carter, ca. 1875.

63. Relief Society Minutes, Minute Book "A," July 1, 1875, Thirteenth Ward, Salt Lake Stake, LDS Church Archives. Photograph courtesy Utah State Historical Society. Charles W. Carter, 1875.

64. Photograph courtesy LDS Church Archives. Charles W. Carter, ca. 1875.

65. "An account of the funeral service of President Brigham Young," given by John Farr, March 1949, microfilm of a typescript, LDS Church Archives. Photograph courtesy LDS Church Archives, Charles W. Carter, 1877.

66. Photograph courtesy LDS Church Archives. Charles R. Savage, 1876.

67. Photograph courtesy LDS Church Archives. F. I. Monsen and Company, ca. 1885.

PART THREE: *1878–1901*

1. *Woman's Exponent,* 1 (July 15, 1872), 29. Photograph courtesy LDS Church Archives. C. M. Bell, 1879.

2. Bryant S. Hinckley, *Heber J. Grant: Highlights in the Life of a Great Leader* (Salt Lake City: Deseret Book Company, 1951), 37–39. Photograph courtesy Kenneth Cannon II. Charles R. Savage, 1878.

3. Photograph courtesy LDS Church Archives. Unknown, ca. 1880.

4. Photograph courtesy LDS Church Archives. Unknown, ca. 1880.

5. Thomas Cott Griggs Journal, May 24, 1880, Microfilm of holograph, LDS Church Archives. Photograph courtesy LDS Church Archives. Unknown, 1880.

6. Photograph courtesy LDS Church Archives. Charles R. Savage, ca. 1883.

7. Photograph courtesy LDS Church Archives. Unknown, ca. 1884.

8. Photograph courtesy LDS Church Archives. Unknown, ca. 1884,

9. Photograph courtesy Scott Christensen. Unknown, ca. 1883.

10. Lundberg family reminiscences, "An Experience of Carl Hendrick Lundberg" [n.d.], microfilm of typescript, LDS Church Archives. Photograph courtesy LDS Church Archives. Unknown, n.d.

11. Photograph courtesy LDS Church Archives. Charles R. Savage, 1884.

12. Photograph courtesy LDS Church Archives. Unknown, ca. 1885.

13. *Dr. Karl G. Maeser Memorial: Tributes from His Students* (Provo, Utah: Brigham Young University, 1907), [13]. Photograph courtesy LDS Church Archives. Thomas E. Daniels, ca. 1885.

14. B. H. Roberts, *The Life of John Taylor* (Salt Lake City: Bookcraft, 1989), 450–51. Photograph courtesy LDS Church Archives. Charles W. Carter, 1887.

15. Nelle Spilsbury Hatch, *Colonia Juarez: An Intimate Account of a Mormon Village* (Salt Lake City: Deseret Book Company, 1954), 73–74. Photograph courtesy LDS Church Archives. Unknown, ca. 1887.

16. Photograph courtesy LDS Church Archives. Charles W. Carter, 1888.

17. Photograph courtesy Utah State Historical Society. George Edward Anderson, 1887.

18. Photograph courtesy LDS Church Archives. Charles R. Savage, ca. 1887.

19. M. Hamlin Cannon, "The Prison Diary of a Mormon Apostle," *Pacific Historical Review* (1947): 399–400. Photograph courtesy LDS Church Archives. C. E. Johnson, 1888.

20. Rudger Clawson, "Personal Experience in the Utah Penitentiary" [n.d.], microfilm of typescript, LDS Church Archives. John Lee Jones Reminiscence [ca. 1900–1926], Carbon copy of typescript, LDS Church Archives. Photograph courtesy LDS Church Archives. Unknown, n.d.

21. Wilford Woodruff Journal, July 8, 1847 (near Ft. Bridger, Wyoming), microfilm of holograph, LDS Church Archives. Photograph courtesy LDS Church Archives. Unknown, 1989.

22. Photograph and information courtesy Jay Burrup. Unknown, ca. 1889.

23. Priesthood Minutes, November 29, 1890, Irish District, Irish Mission; Historical Records and Minutes, December 31, 1890, Irish District, Irish Mission, LDS Church Archives. Photograph courtesy LDS Church Archives. Lee, 1890.

24. Rigby Family History [ca. 1890–1983], microfilm of typescript, Rigby Family Collection, LDS Church Archives. Photograph courtesy LDS Church Archives. Charles R. Savage, 1890.

25. Wilford Woodruff Journal, April 6, 1892, microfilm of holograph, LDS Church Archives. Photograph courtesy LDS Church Archives. Sainsbury and Johnson, 1893.

26. Photograph courtesy Utah State Historical Society. Charles W. Carter, 1892.

27. Wilford Woodruff Journal, February 8, 1893, microfilm of holograph, LDS Church Archives. Photograph courtesy LDS Church Archives. Unknown, 1892.

28. Olive Middleton Holding, "Pioneer Ephraim George Holding," (unpublished, Daughters of the Utah Pioneers, Camp 21: 1946), [2]. Photograph courtesy Sheri Eardley Slaughter. Mikkel A. Faldmo, 1893.

29. Wilford Woodruff journal, April 6, 1893, microfilm of holograph, LDS Church Archives. Photograph courtesy LDS Church Archives. Sainsbury and Johnson, 1893.

30. Photograph courtesy Utah State Historical Society. Unknown, n.d.

31. Photograph courtesy LDS Church Archives. Charles R. Savage, ca. 1893.

32. Photograph courtesy Special Collections, University of Utah. Unknown, 1894.

33. Photograph courtesy Utah State Historical Society. Unknown, 1895.

34. As quoted in Ellis Shipp Musser, comp., *The Early Autobiography and Diary of Ellis Reynolds Shipp, M.D.* (Salt Lake City: Deseret News Press, 1962), vi. Photograph courtesy LDS Church Archives. Unknown, 1896.

35. Photograph courtesy LDS Church Archives. M. Walter Batty, 1895.

36. Charles B. Stewart diary, private possession. Use courtesy David H. Epperson. Photograph courtesy Utah State Historical Society. C. E. Johnson, 1896.

37. Photograph courtesy LDS Church Archives. Unknown, 1896.

38. As quoted in Janet Burton Seegmiller, *"Be Kind to the Poor": The Life Story of Robert Taylor Burton* (Robert Taylor Burton Family Organization, 1988), 409. Photograph courtesy LDS Church Archives. Unknown, 1896.

39. Photograph courtesy Special Collections, University of Utah. Unknown, 1896.

40. Photograph courtesy Utah State Historical Society. R. M. Robinson, 1897.

41. Olive Wood Nielson, *A Treasury of Edward J. Wood* (Salt Lake City: Publisher's Press, 1983), 191, 200. Photograph courtesy LDS Church Archives. Unknown, ca. 1896.

42. Erwin G. Gudde, *Bigler's Chronicle of the West* (Berkeley: University of California Press, 1962), 87–89. Photograph courtesy LDS Church Archives. Unknown, 1898.

43. San Juan Stake, Relief Society Minutes, June 12, 1889 to June 1899, microfilm of holograph, LDS Church Archives. Photograph courtesy Utah State Historical Society. Unknown, ca. 1898.

44. As quoted in Melvin Bashore and Scott Crump, *Riverton: The Story of a Utah Country Town* (Riverton, Utah: Riverton Historical Society, 1994), 382. Photograph courtesy Sheri Eardley Slaughter. Fox and Symons, 1899.

45. *Deseret Evening News,* April 16, 1898, 18. Photograph courtesy LDS Church Archives. Johnson Company, 1898.

46. Matthias F. Cowley, *Wilford Woodruff: History of His Life and Labors* (Salt Lake City: Deseret News Press, 1909), 622. Photograph courtesy Utah State Historical Society. Unknown, 1898.

47. Photograph courtesy LDS Church Archives. Unknown, 1898.

48. Harrison R. Merrill, "Dave Rust, Lover of the Grand Canyon," *Improvement Era* 32 (April 1929): 473. Photograph courtesy LDS Church Archives. N. Galloway, 1899.

49. Photograph courtesy LDS Church Archives. N. Galloway, 1899.

50. Photograph courtesy Utah State Historical Society. Unknown, 1899.

51. Photograph courtesy LDS Church Archives. Unknown, 1899.

52. "Our Missionary Work," *Improvement Era* 1 (December 1897): 139. Photograph courtesy LDS Church Archives. Charles R. Savage, 1899.

53. Charles A. Welch, *History of the Big Horn Basin* (Salt Lake City: Deseret News Press, 1940), 71. Photograph courtesy LDS Church Archives. J. H. Cutler, 1900.

54. Photograph courtesy LDS Church Archives. Fox and Symons, 1900.

55. Photograph courtesy LDS Church Archives. Matson and Christenson, ca. 1900.

56. Thomas Romney, *The Life of Lorenzo Snow* (Salt Lake City: Deseret News Press, 1955), 14–15. Photograph courtesy Utah State Historical Society. Unknown, ca. 1901.

PART FOUR: *1902–1945*

1. As quoted in Francis M. Gibbons, *Heber J. Grant: Man of Steel, Prophet of God* (Salt Lake City: Deseret Book Company, 1979), 116–17. Photograph courtesy Utah State Historical Society. Unknown, ca. 1902.

2. Information supplied on back of photograph. Photograph courtesy Utah State Historical Society. Unknown, 1902.

3. Jean Bickmore White, ed., *Church, State, and Politics: The Diaries of John Henry Smith* (Salt Lake City: Signature Books, 1990), 522. Photograph courtesy LDS Church Archives. Unknown, 1903.

4. Ella Wheeler Wilcox, *The Worlds and I* (New York: George H. Doran Company, 1918), 310–12. Photograph courtesy LDS Church Archives. Unknown, 1903.

5. "'Old Folks' Excursions," Kate B. Carter, comp. *Our Pioneer Heritage,* 20 vols. (Salt Lake City: Daughters of the Utah Pioneers, 1858–1977), 19:2. Photograph courtesy LDS Church Archives. Charles R. Savage Co., 1903.

6. Photograph courtesy LDS Church Archives. Underwood and Underwood, 1904.

7. As quoted in Albert R. Lyman, "Aunt Jody, Nurse of the San Juan Frontier," *Improvement Era* 61 (September 1958): 652. Photograph courtesy Utah State Historical Society. Unknown, ca. 1905.

8. Photograph courtesy LDS Church Archives. Unknown, 1905.

9. Photograph courtesy Utah State Historical Society. William Shipler, 1906.

10. Photograph courtesy Utah State Historical Society. Charles R. Savage Co., 1905.

11. As quoted in Gibbons, *Heber J. Grant,* 143. Photograph courtesy LDS Church Archives. Unknown, 1906.

12. Information and photograph courtesy Sheri E. Slaughter. Unknown, 1907.

13. Photograph of tintype courtesy LDS Church Archives. Unknown, ca. 1908.

14. Information and photograph courtesy Sheri E. Slaughter. Unknown, 1910.

15. Joseph Henry Stimpson Journal, October 11, 1908, microfilm of holograph, Joseph Henry Stimpson Collection, LDS Church Archives. Photograph courtesy LDS Church Archives. Joseph H. Stimpson, 1908.

16. Photograph courtesy LDS Church Archives. Unknown, ca. 1910.

17. Photograph courtesy LDS Church Archives. Unknown, 1909.

18. Photograph courtesy LDS Church Archives. C. R. Savage Co., ca. 1911.

19. As quoted in Thomas Cottam Romney, *The Mormon Colonies in Mexico* (Salt Lake City: Deseret Book Company, 1938), 190. Photograph courtesy LDS Church Archives. Unknown, 1912.

20. Photograph courtesy LDS Church Archives. Unknown, 1912.

21. Photograph courtesy LDS Church Archives. Olson and Hafen, 1911.

22. Photograph courtesy LDS Church Archives. C. E. Johnson, 1913.

23. Information and photograph courtesy Jay G. Burrup. Unknown, 1907.

24. Information and photograph courtesy Jay G. Burrup. Unknown, 1913.

25. As quoted in Edward L. Kimball and Andrew E. Kimball, Jr., *Spencer W. Kimball: Twelfth President of The Church of Jesus Christ of Latter-day Saints* (Salt Lake City: Bookcraft, 1977), 76–77. Photograph courtesy LDS Church. Unknown, ca. 1914.

26. As quoted in Joseph Fielding Smith, comp., *Life of Joseph F. Smith* (Salt Lake City: Deseret News Press, 1938), 449. Photograph courtesy LDS Church Archives. Unknown, 1914.

27. As quoted in Robert H. Malan, *B. H. Roberts: A Biography* (Salt Lake City: Deseret Book Company, 1966), 107. Photograph courtesy LDS Church Archives. Unknown, 1917.

28. Photograph and information courtesy Mae Timbimboo Parry. Unknown, 1918.

29. Photograph courtesy LDS Church Archives. Unknown, 1922.

30. Photograph courtesy Special Collections, University of Utah. Unknown, 1922.

31. Photograph courtesy LDS Church Archives. Unknown, ca. 1922.

32. Photograph courtesy LDS Church Archives. Antoine Bunker, ca. 1923.

33. As quoted in Olive Wood Nielson, *A Treasury of Edward J. Wood* (Salt Lake City: Publisher's Press, 1983), 473. Photograph courtesy LDS Church Archives. George Edward Anderson, 1923.

34. As quoted in *A Treasury of Edward J. Wood,* 474, 476. Photograph courtesy LDS Church Archives. Unknown, 1923.

35. As quoted in William T. Black, *Mormon Athletes: Book 2* (Salt Lake City: Deseret Book Company, 1982), 221. Photograph courtesy Utah State Historical Society. Unknown, ca. 1924.

36. Photograph courtesy Utah State Historical Society. Unknown, 1924.

37. "Biographical sketch of Evan Stephens" [n.d.], microfilm of typescript, LDS Church Archives. Photograph courtesy LDS Church Archives. Unknown, ca. 1925.

38. James Vernon Sharp Journal, June 7, 1927, microfilm of holograph, LDS Church Archives. Photograph courtesy LDS Church Archives. Unknown, 1927.

39. Photograph courtesy LDS Church Archives. Unknown, ca. 1926.

40. M. Kip Hartvigsen, *Goodly Parents: Life Sketches of Milton Farrell and Virgil Burrup Hartvigsen* (privately published, 1987), 39. Photograph courtesy Jay G. Burrup. Unknown, ca. 1927.

41. Photograph courtesy LDS Church Archives. Unknown, 1928.

42. Photograph courtesy LDS Church Archives. Unknown, 1927.

43. Photograph courtesy Utah State Historical Society. Unknown, 1928.

44. Photograph courtesy LDS Church Archives. Unknown, ca. 1928.

45. As quoted in Carolyn W. D. Pearson, "Susa Young Gates," *Mormon Sisters: Women in Early Utah,* edited by Claudia L. Bushman (Salt Lake City: Olympus Publishing Co., 1976), 219. Photograph courtesy Utah State Historical Society. Unknown, ca. 1932.

46. Photograph courtesy LDS Church Archives. Unknown, 1931.

47. As quoted in Wendell J. Ashton, "Gordon B. Hinckley of the Quorum of the Twelve," *Improvement Era* 64 (December 1961): 907. Photograph courtesy LDS Church Archives. Unknown, ca. 1935.

48. As quoted in Spencer W. Kimball, *Conference Report* (October 1977): 123. Photograph courtesy LDS Church Archives. Unknown, 1936.

49. C. Lucius Laudie to R. W. Eardley, October 21, 1938, Correspondence, Welfare Photograph Collection, LDS Church Archives. Photograph courtesy the LDS Church Archives. Unknown, 1938.

50. "Church News Section," *Deseret News* (August 7, 1937): 2. Photograph courtesy LDS Church Archives. Unknown, 1937.

51. As quoted in L. Brent Goates, *Harold B. Lee: Prophet and Seer* (Salt Lake City: Bookcraft, 1985), 114–15. Photograph courtesy LDS Church Archives. Unknown, ca. 1938.

52. "Church News Section," *Deseret News* (July 2, 1938): 7. Photograph courtesy LDS Church Archives. Unknown, 1938.

53. Photograph courtesy Utah State Historical Society. Bill Shipler, 1940.

54. Photograph courtesy Special Collections, University of Utah. Unknown, 1941.

55. Information and photograph courtesy Jay G. Burrup. Unknown, 1942.

56. Photograph courtesy Utah State Historical Society. Unknown, 1943.

57. Photograph courtesy LDS Church Archives. Unknown, 1943.

58. Photograph courtesy LDS Church Archives. W. A. MacDonald, 1944.

59. Information and photograph courtesy Jay G. Burrup. Unknown, 1944.

60. George Frederick Poole, interview, typescript, 1987, James Moyle Oral History Program, LDS Church Archives. Photograph courtesy LDS Church Archives. Unknown, ca. 1945.

PART FIVE: *1945–1995*

1. As quoted in Merlo J. Pusey, *Builders of the Kingdom* (Provo: Brigham Young University Press, 1981), 361. Photograph courtesy Utah State Historical Society. Unknown, ca. 1945.

2. Information and photograph courtesy Special Collections, University of Utah. Unknown, 1945.

3. Photograph courtesy Utah State Historical Society. *Deseret News*, 1947.

4. *Church News*, December 6, 1947, 1. Photograph courtesy LDS Church Archives. Unknown, 1947.

5. As quoted in Susan Arrington Madsen, *I Walked to Zion: True Stories of Young Pioneers on the Mormon Trail* (Salt Lake City: Deseret Book Company, 1994), 139. Photograph courtesy LDS Church Archives. Unknown, 1947.

6. Photograph courtesy LDS Church Archives. Unknown, 1948.

7. Photograph courtesy Utah State Historical Society. Unknown, ca. 1951.

8. As quoted in Heidi S. Swinton, *In the Company of Prophets* (Salt Lake City: Deseret Book Company, 1993), 115. Photograph courtesy LDS Church. U.S. Department of Agriculture photographer, ca. 1953.

9. As quoted in Francis M. Gibbons, *Joseph Fielding Smith: Gospel Scholar, Prophet of God* (Salt Lake City: Deseret Book Company, 1992), 399–400. Photograph courtesy LDS Church Archives. Utah Air National Guard, 1954.

10. As quoted in L. Brent Goates, *Harold B. Lee: Prophet and Seer* (Salt Lake City: Bookcraft, 1985), 247–48. Photograph courtesy LDS Church Archives. U.S. Army, 1954.

11. Photograph courtesy LDS Church Archives. Eddy Van Der Veen, ca. 1955.

12. Information and photograph courtesy Jay G. Burrup. Unknown, 1957.

13. Photograph courtesy LDS Church Archives. Lee Van Photo, 1958.

14. Photograph courtesy LDS Church Archives. Myrtle Deborah McDonald, 1958.

15. Janet Peterson and LaRene Gaunt, *Elect Ladies* (Salt Lake City: Deseret Book Company, 1990), 161–62. Photograph courtesy Utah State Historical Society. Unknown, 1959.

16. Quotation and photograph courtesy Ronald G. Watt. Ronald G. Watt, 1960.

17. Information and photograph courtesy Jay G. Burrup. Unknown, 1960.

18. Photograph courtesy Ronald G. Watt. Ronald G. Watt, 1961.

19. *Deseret News-Telegram*, September 26, 1963, 6, 10. Photograph courtesy LDS Church. Unknown, 1963.

20. As quoted in David Lawrence McKay, *My Father: David O. McKay* edited by Lavina Fielding Anderson (Salt Lake City: Deseret Book Company, 1989), 121. Photograph courtesy LDS Church Archives. Unknown, n.d.

21. Information and photograph courtesy Jay G. Burrup. Unknown, 1964.

22. Information with the photograph. Photograph courtesy LDS Church Archives. Unknown, 1969.

23. Joseph Fielding McConkie, "Joseph Fielding Smith," *The Presidents of the Church,* edited by Leonard J. Arrington (Salt Lake City: Deseret Book Company, 1986), 339–40. Photograph courtesy LDS Church Archives. Eldon Linschoten, ca. 1970.

24. As quoted in Goates, *Harold B. Lee,* 497. Photograph courtesy Utah State Historical Society. Unknown, 1972.

25. Spencer W. Kimball, *Official Report of the Fiji Area Conference* (Salt Lake City: The Church of Jesus Christ of Latter-day Saints, 1976), 1. Photograph courtesy LDS Church Archives. Fiji Sun, 1976.

26. Dr. Norman Vincent Peale, "Remarks at President Kimball's Eighty-fifth Birthday Dinner, 28 March 1980," *Ensign* 10 (May 1980): 109. Photograph courtesy LDS Church Archives. Unknown, n.d.

27. Information and photograph courtesy Jay G. Burrup. Jay G. Burrup, 1977.

28. Official Declaration–2. Photograph courtesy LDS Church Archives. Robert W. Stum, ca. 1988.

29. Pres. Reagan sees how LDS care for own," *Church News,* September 18, 1982, 3, 8. Photograph courtesy LDS Church Archives. U.S. White House photographer, 1982.

30. Information and photograph courtesy Scott R. Christensen. Darren Klein, 1983.

31. Photograph courtesy LDS Church Archives. Gerry Avant, 1983.

32. Photograph courtesy LDS Church Archives. Unknown, 1989.

33. Gordon B. Hinckley, *Conference Report* (October 6, 1985), 72. Photograph courtesy Matthew K. Heiss. Matthew K. Heiss, 1991.

34. Dell Van Orden and Gerry Avant, "A new day dawns on African nations," *Church News,* October 17, 1987, 10. Photograph courtesy LDS Church Archives. Robert W. Stum, 1988.

35. Photograph courtesy LDS Church Archives. Claire J. Fisher, 1988.

36. Information courtesy Scott Christensen. Photograph courtesy Chris Elggren. Chris Elggren, 1990.

37. Photograph courtesy Gerry Avant. Gerry Avant, 1991.

38. Photograph courtesy LDS Church Archives. Unknown, n.d.

39. Photograph courtesy LDS Church Archives. Jack Monson, n.d.

CHRONOLOGY

1820 The First Vision: the Father and the Son visited Joseph Smith.

1827 Joseph Smith received the gold plates from which the Book of Mormon was translated.

Ludwig von Beethoven died of pneumonia at age fifty-six.

1829 In May, Joseph Smith and Oliver Cowdery received the Aaronic Priesthood from John the Baptist.

In May or June, Joseph Smith and Oliver Cowdery had the Melchizedek Priesthood conferred upon them by Peter, James, and John.

1830 The first edition of the Book of Mormon was published in March.

On April 6 the Church of Christ was organized.

Mountain men Jedediah Smith and William Sublette of the Rocky Mountain Fur Company led the first covered wagons from the Missouri River into the Rocky Mountains.

1831 By May the majority of the Saints moved to the Kirtland, Ohio, area.

The Prophet Joseph Smith began moving members to Jackson County, Missouri, the New Jerusalem.

In both Kirtland and Jackson County, the Saints were heavily persecuted.

King Louis Philippe created the elite French Foreign Legion.

1832 Missionaries went into Canada, the first missionary effort outside the United States.

1833 In Kirtland, Joseph Smith received the revelation known as the Word of Wisdom.

The First Presidency was organized; Sidney Rigdon and Frederick G. Williams were called to be counselors to Joseph Smith.

Because of mob persecution, the Saints left Jackson County, Missouri.

Slavery was abolished in the British Empire.

1834 The first high council was organized.

At a conference in Kirtland, the Church was named "The Church of the Latter-day Saints."

"Zion's Camp" marched from Ohio to Missouri to assist persecuted Missouri Saints.

1835 Twelve apostles were chosen by the Three Witnesses to the Book of Mormon.

The First Quorum of Seventy was organized.

Hans Christian Andersen published the first of his 168 fairytales, Tales Told for Children.

1836 The Kirtland Temple, the first temple of this dispensation, was dedicated in March.

In April the Savior, Moses, Elias, and Elijah appeared to Joseph Smith and Oliver Cowdery in the Kirtland Temple and gave them the keys of each of their dispensations.

1837 First missionaries were sent to Great Britain in June.

In July nine persons were baptized in the River Ribble, Preston, England.

Eighteen-year-old Princess Victoria became queen of the United Kingdom (Great Britain).

1838 Exodus from Kirtland, Ohio.

The name of the Church was changed to "The Church of Jesus Christ of Latter-day Saints."

In July the law of tithing was given at Far West, Missouri.

In October Missouri governor Lilburn Boggs issued an "exterminate or expel" order against the Saints; the Haun's Mill Massacre occurred; Joseph Smith and others were arrested by militia.

In December Joseph Smith and others began a six-month imprisonment in Liberty Jail.

The Cherokees were forced from their homeland in Georgia and were brutally marched west to what is now Oklahoma. This forced exodus was heavy with loss of life and became known as the "trail of tears."

1839 Brigham Young removed the Saints to Illinois.

Joseph Smith and others were released from Liberty Jail in April.

Commerce, Illinois, was selected as the next gathering place for the Saints; its name was changed to Nauvoo.

In France, Louis Daguerre introduced the first usable photographic process, the daguerreotype.

1840 Converts from Europe began immigrating to the United States.

The "Nauvoo Charter" bill was signed into law by Illinois governor Thomas Carlin.

Upper and lower Canada were united.

1841 Baptism for the dead was introduced as a temple ordinance.

The cornerstone was laid for the Nauvoo Temple.

1842 The Female Relief Society was organized in Nauvoo. The Articles of Faith were published for the first time in the *Times and Seasons.*

In May the Prophet revealed the temple endowment.

1843 A revelation on the "Eternity of the Marriage Covenant and Plural Marriage" was received.

Charles Dickens published A Christmas Carol.

1844 On June 27 the Prophet Joseph Smith and his brother Hyrum were murdered at Carthage Jail.

In August Brigham Young and the Twelve were sustained by vote to lead the Church.

Samuel Morse transmitted the first telegraph message from Washington, D.C., to Baltimore, Maryland.

1846 The westward migration of the Saints began in February.

The ship *Brooklyn* left New York City bound for California.

Temporary settlements were established at Mt. Pisgah, Iowa; Council Bluffs, Iowa; and Winter Quarters, Nebraska.

In July the Mormon Battalion was organized and left for Fort Leavenworth.

The United States declared war on Mexico.

1847 The first pioneer wagon companies arrived in the Salt Lake Valley on July 24.

In December Brigham Young was sustained as president of the Church.

1848 Mormon Battalion members were at Sutter's Mill, California, when gold was discovered.

Seagulls devoured the millions of crickets that were ruining the pioneers' crops.

1849 The Perpetual Emigration Fund was established to help the poor come to Utah.

1850 Utah was made a territory with Brigham Young as governor.

1851 *Isaac M. Singer was granted a patent for the first continuous-stitch sewing machine for domestic use.*

1852 The doctrine of polygamy was publicly announced.

1853 The Salt Lake Temple site was dedicated in February, and the cornerstone laid in April.

1854 *Henry David Thoreau published* Walden.

1856 The first handcart companies left Iowa City, Iowa. The Willie and Martin handcart disasters occurred.

Gail Borden patented condensed milk in the United States.

1857 Apostle Parley P. Pratt was murdered in Arkansas.

The Mountain Meadows Massacre tragedy took place in September.

Johnston's Army (federal troops) tried and failed to enter Salt Lake City.

Elisha Otis installed the first passenger elevator in a New York department store.

1858 In June federal troops peacefully entered Salt Lake City.

1860 The last companies to use handcarts arrived in Salt Lake City in September.

1861 The transcontinental telegraph was joined in Salt Lake City.

The Civil War began when Confederate forces fired on Fort Sumter, South Carolina.

1862 The Salt Lake Theatre was dedicated.

The U.S. Congress declared polygamy a crime.

1863 *President Abraham Lincoln signed the Emancipation Proclamation, freeing all slaves in the United States.*

1865 Fighting erupted with Indians in central Utah; it was known as the Black Hawk War.

President Abraham Lincoln was assassinated by John Wilkes Booth.

1866 The *Juvenile Instructor* began publication as the organ of the Sunday School.

1867 Brigham Young requested bishops to reorganize ward Relief Societies, which had been disbanded during the Utah War.

October general conference was the first held in the newly completed Tabernacle.

1869 In May the transcontinental railroads were joined at Promontory, Utah.

ZCMI opened its doors for business.

The Young Ladies' Retrenchment Association was formed, later renamed the Young Women's Mutual Improvement Association.

The Suez Canal opened for traffic, connecting the Mediterranean Sea with the Red Sea.

1872 The *Woman's Exponent* began publication, continuing until 1914.

Yellowstone National Park was established by act of Congress.

1875 The first Young Men's Mutual Improvement Association began in the Thirteenth Ward.

Brigham Young University was founded.

1876 A central committee was formed to coordinate all YMMIAs.

Alexander Graham Bell was granted a patent for the telephone.

1877 On April 6 the St. George Temple was dedicated.

On August 29 Brigham Young died.

The Quorum of the Twelve, with John Taylor at the head, assumed leadership of the Church.

1878 The first Mormon settlement in Colorado was founded in Conejos County.

The Primary was founded by Aurelia Rogers.

1879 The first edition of the *Contributor,* organ of the YMMIA, was published. It continued until 1896.

Thomas Edison invented the lightbulb.

1880 In October John Taylor was sustained as president of the Church.

1881	*The American Red Cross was organized.*
1882	The Edmunds antipolygamy bill became law. Many men were imprisoned because of it.
1883	The first Maori branch was organized in New Zealand.
	The United States Civil Service System was established.
1884	The Logan Temple was dedicated on May 17.
	Construction began on the first skyscraper, the Home Insurance Company, Chicago.
1885	President John Taylor and others went into hiding to avoid antipolygamy harassment.
1886	The first LDS meetinghouse was built and used in Colonia Juarez.
	The Statue of Liberty, a gift from France, was dedicated in New York Harbor.
1887	The Edmunds-Tucker Act became law, toughening the 1882 antipolygamy bill.
	Cardston, Alberta, Canada, was established by the Latter-day Saints.
	President John Taylor died on July 25. The Council of the Twelve assumed leadership of the Church.
1888	The Manti Temple was dedicated.
	The first authorized missionary was sent to Samoa.
	George Eastman introduced the first simple, inexpensive camera, the Kodak.
1889	In April Wilford Woodruff was sustained as president of the Church.
1890	President Wilford Woodruff issued the "Manifesto," which officially ended the practice of polygamy by the Church.
1892	*Jesse Reno was granted a patent for the first escalator.*
1893	U.S. President Benjamin Harrison issued a proclamation of amnesty to all polygamists who entered marriage before November 1, 1890.
	On April 6 the Salt Lake Temple was dedicated.
1894	The Genealogical Society of Utah was organized.
1896	Utah was granted statehood.
1897	The *Improvement Era* began publication, continuing until 1970.
1898	President Wilford Woodruff died on September 2.
	On September 13 Lorenzo Snow became the fifth president of the Church.
	Spain declared war on the United States.
1901	Heber J. Grant dedicated Japan for missionary work.
	Lorenzo Snow died on October 10.
	Joseph F. Smith was ordained president of the Church.
	Queen Victoria died. Her son, Edward VII, became king of the United Kingdom.
1902	The *Children's Friend*, a magazine for Primary children, began publication. It was replaced by the *Friend* in 1970.
1903	*The Wright brothers flew their "Flyer" at Kitty Hawk, North Carolina.*
1905	*Twenty-six-year-old Albert Einstein published his "theory of relativity."*
1906	President Joseph F. Smith visited Europe, the first president in office to do so.
	An earthquake measuring 8.25 on the Richter Scale leveled 490 city blocks in San Francisco.
1907	The U.S. Senate agreed to seat Utah senator and apostle Reed Smoot after three years of investigation into polygamy.
1908	*Henry Ford's first Model T automobile rolled off the assembly line in Detroit.*
1911	The Church adopted the Boy Scout program.
	Theodore Roosevelt wrote a letter to *Collier's* magazine defending Senator Reed Smoot and the Church.
1912	The first seminary opened at Salt Lake City's Granite High School.
	The Correlation Committee was created.
	The "unsinkable" Titanic *sank on its maiden voyage from England to New York City.*
1913	The Boy Scout program was integrated with YMMIA.
1914	The *Relief Society* magazine was founded. It ceased publication in 1970 when the *Ensign* was created.
	World War I began with the assassination of Archduke Francis Ferdinand, heir to the Austro-Hungarian throne.
1915	*Jesus the Christ,* by James Talmage, was published.
1917	The Church Administration Building was completed.
	Bolsheviks overthrew Kerensky in the Russian government. The United States declared war on the Central Powers (Austria-Hungary, Germany, and Turkey).
1918	The Relief Society sold its stored wheat to the U.S. government to aid in the war effort of World War I.
	Joseph F. Smith died on November 19. No public funeral was held because of the worldwide influenza epidemic.
	Heber J. Grant was sustained as president on November 23.
	World War I ended with the surrender of Germany.
1919	The Hawaii Temple was dedicated on November 27.
	The 18th amendment to the United States Constitution established prohibition; the amendment was repealed in 1933.
1920	The First Presidency sent Elder David O. McKay and Liberty Stake president Hugh J. Cannon on a worldwide tour to visit members and missions; they visited the Pacific Islands, Australia, New Zealand, Asia, India, the Middle East, and Europe.
	American women received the right to vote with the passage of the 19th amendment to the United States Constitution.

1922   The Primary Children's Hospital opened in Salt Lake City.

1923   The Alberta Temple was dedicated on August 26 in Cardston, Canada.

1924   KSL began radio broadcasts of general conference.

1925   Apostle Melvin J. Ballard opened South America for missionary work.

Nellie Taylor Ross of Wyoming became the first woman governor of a state as she completed the unexpired term of her husband.

1926   The first institute opened at the University of Idaho, Moscow, Idaho.

A. A. Milne published Winnie-the-Pooh.

1927   The Arizona (Mesa) Temple was dedicated on October 23.

Charles Lindbergh successfully completed a nonstop, solo flight from New York to Paris.

1929   The Tabernacle Choir started a weekly national radio broadcast on NBC. A year later Richard L. Evans joined them with his sermonettes. Eventually "Music and the Spoken Word" switched to KSL/CBS.

The New York Stock Market crashed amid a flurry of trading and ushered in the Great Depression.

1931   The "Church News" section of the *Deseret News* was first published.

1933   *Adolf Hitler was named chancellor of Germany.*

1934   *Adolf Hitler took control of Germany upon the death of President Paul von Hindenburg.*

1936   The Church Welfare Program was introduced.

1937   President Heber J. Grant toured Europe for three months, visiting members and missionaries.

The first Deseret Industries opened in Salt Lake City.

1939   Missionaries in Germany were notified to move to neutral countries.

World War II began when Nazi Germany invaded Poland.

1940   Church membership numbered 862,000.

1941   The position of Assistant to the Quorum of the Twelve was created.

The Japanese attacked the American fleet anchored at Pearl Harbor, Hawaii. This act brought the United States into World War II.

1942   The Church restricted auxiliary and general board meetings to help comply with wartime travel restrictions.

For the duration of the war, only older men were called on full-time missions.

As of April, attendance at general conference was restricted to General Authorities and stake presidencies; the Tabernacle was closed for the duration of the war to aid with national resource limitations.

The USS *Brigham Young* was launched.

1943   The USS *Joseph Smith* was launched.

1945   President Heber J. Grant died on May 14.

George Albert Smith was set apart as president on May 21.

Mission presidents were called and sent to areas abandoned during the war.

The Tabernacle was opened to general conference in October.

May 7 became Victory in Europe Day as Germany's armed forces surrendered to the Allies.

September 2: Japanese officials signed papers of unconditional surrender.

1946   The Church sent material aid to the Saints in Europe.

1947   Church membership exceeded 1 million.

1949   The first public television broadcast of general conference was aired in October.

1950   The first early morning seminaries began in Southern California.

The Korean War began.

1951   On April 4 President George Albert Smith passed away.

On April 9 David O. McKay became the ninth president of the Church.

Color TV was introduced in the United States.

1952   President David O. McKay toured Europe for six weeks.

U.S. President Dwight D. Eisenhower chose apostle Ezra Taft Benson as U.S. Secretary of Agriculture.

1953   *Edmund Hillary and Tenzing Norkay became the first climbers to successfully scale Mt. Everest.*

1954   The Indian Placement Program began.

1955   President McKay visited missions and members in the South Pacific.

The Northern Far East and Southern Far East missions were organized.

On September 11 the Swiss Temple was dedicated—the first European temple.

1956   On March 11 the Los Angeles Temple was dedicated.

The Relief Society Building was dedicated on October 3.

1957   *The Soviet Union put the first man-made satellite into orbit; the Space Age began.*

1958   The New Zealand Temple was dedicated on April 20.

The London Temple was dedicated on September 7.

1959   *Hawaii was admitted to the Union as the fiftieth state.*

1961   The Language Training Institute was established at BYU.

The "Every member a missionary" program was introduced.

1962   The first Spanish-speaking stake was organized in Mexico City.

John Glenn became the first American to orbit the earth.

1963   The Polynesian Cultural Center opened in Hawaii.

United States president John F. Kennedy was assassinated in Dallas Texas.

1964   The Oakland Temple was dedicated on November 17.

1965   The Tabernacle Choir sang at the inauguration of U.S. President Lyndon B. Johnson.

Italy was officially opened to missionary work.

1966   The first stake in South America was organized in São Paulo, Brazil.

1967   *Israel swiftly defeated Egypt in the "Six-Day War."*

1968   Relief Society president Belle Spafford became president of the National Council of Women.

Civil rights leader and nonviolence advocate Martin Luther King was gunned down in Memphis, Tennessee.

1969   *United States astronaut Neil Armstrong became the first human to walk on the moon. His famous words: "That's one small step for a man, one giant leap for mankind."*

1970   President David O. McKay died on January 18.

On January 23 Joseph Fielding Smith became president of the Church.

The first stake in Asia was formed in Tokyo.

The first stake in Africa was organized in South Africa.

The first Earth Day was celebrated to call attention to the fragile condition of the earth.

1971   The *Ensign,* the *New Era,* and the *Friend* began publication.

The first area conference was held in Manchester, England.

1972   The Ogden Temple was dedicated on January 18.

The Provo Temple was dedicated on February 9.

President Joseph Fielding Smith died on July 2.

On July 7 Harold B. Lee became the eleventh president of the Church.

Church administrative departments moved into the new twenty-eight-story Church Office Building.

1973   The first Church agricultural missionaries were sent to South America.

Church membership reached 3 million.

President Harold B. Lee died on December 26.

On December 30 Spencer W. Kimball was set apart as president of the Church.

1974   The names of stakes throughout the Church were changed to a consistent style to reflect geographic localities.

The Washington (D.C.) Temple was dedicated November 19.

United States president Richard Nixon resigned from office in the face of certain impeachment.

1975   The area supervisory program was announced.

The First Quorum of the Seventy was organized.

The Vietnam War ended with the occupation of Saigon by Communist troops.

1978   Announcement of the revelation making worthy males of all races eligible for the priesthood.

The São Paulo (Brazil) Temple was dedicated on October 30.

1979   The 1,000th stake was created at Nauvoo, Illinois.

President Kimball toured the Middle East and dedicated the Orson Hyde Memorial Gardens in Israel.

The Church published the LDS edition of the King James Version of the Bible.

The United States and China reestablished diplomatic relations after years of opposition.

1980   U.S. and Canadian members began the consolidated meeting schedule.

The Tokyo Temple was dedicated October 27.

The Seattle Temple was dedicated November 17.

Washington State's Mt. St. Helens erupted.

1981   Plans to build smaller temples in nine areas were announced.

Revised editions of the Book of Mormon, Doctrine and Covenants, and Pearl of Great Price were published.

The Jordan River Temple was dedicated on November 16.

Sandra Day O'Connor was nominated by United States president Ronald Reagan to become the first woman member of the U.S. Supreme Court.

1982   Church membership reached 5 million.

The Mormon Tabernacle Choir celebrated fifty years of broadcasting on CBS.

Dr. Barney Clark became the first recipient of an artificial heart; the operation was performed at the University of Utah Medical Center. Dr. Clark lived for 112 days after receiving the device.

1983   The Atlanta (Georgia) Temple was dedicated June 1–4.

The Apia Samoa Temple was dedicated August 5.

The Nuku'alofa Tonga Temple was dedicated August 9.

The Santiago Chile Temple was dedicated September 15.

The Papeete Tahiti Temple was dedicated October 27.

The Mexico City Temple was dedicated December 2.

1984   The Church's 1,500th stake was formed—the Ciudad Obregan Mexico Yaqui Stake.

The Boise Temple was dedicated May 25.

The Sydney Australia Temple was dedicated September 20.

The Manila Philippines Temple was dedicated September 25.

The Dallas Temple was dedicated October 19.

The Taipei Taiwan Temple was dedicated November 17.

The Guatemala City Temple was dedicated December 14.

Sharlene Wells of Salt Lake City won the "Miss America" title.

1985 BYU's 1984 football team was voted National Champion.

A new hymnal was published.

The Freiberg Germany Temple was dedicated June 29, the first and only temple in a communist Eastern Bloc nation.

The Stockholm Sweden Temple was dedicated July 2.

The Chicago Temple was dedicated August 9.

The Johannesburg Temple was dedicated August 24.

The new Church Genealogical Library opened to the public.

President Spencer W. Kimball died November 5.

Ezra Taft Benson was set apart as president November 10.

The Seoul Korea Temple was dedicated December 14.

1986 Church membership passed the 6 million mark.

The 1,600th stake was organized at Kitchener, Ontario.

The Lima Peru Temple was dedicated January 10.

The Denver Colorado Temple was dedicated October 24.

Robert Penn Warren became the first official poet laureate of the United States.

1987 The Church Genealogical Library converted its last catalog card to computer.

The Genealogical Department was renamed the Family History Department.

The Frankfurt Temple was dedicated August 28.

"Glasnost" (openness) began as Soviet Union leader Mikhail Gorbachev began a series of economic and social reforms in the Communist nation.

1988 Seven new stakes were created in Lima, Peru.

The first stake in which all priesthood leaders were black was organized—the Aba Nigeria Stake.

Hungary officially allowed missionary work.

East Germany granted rights for the Church to send missionaries.

Benazir Bhutto was chosen to be prime minister of Pakistan, the first Islamic woman to fill this position of leadership.

1989 The BYU Jerusalem Center opened.

The Second Quorum of the Seventy was organized.

Mexico's 100th stake was created.

The Portland Oregon Temple was dedicated August 19.

The first LDS chapel in Hungary was dedicated.

A revised ward budget plan was implemented.

The Las Vegas Temple was dedicated December 16.

U. S. Troops invaded Panama and captured General Manuel Noriega.

1990 The Tabernacle Choir toured Europe and the Soviet Union.

New missions opened in Hungary, Poland, and Czechoslovakia.

The Toronto Temple was dedicated August 25.

The Soviet Union gave official approval for the "registration" of the Leningrad Branch.

Church membership numbered more than 7.7 million.

The number of wards and branches reached 15,000.

"Operation Desert Shield" began in August as international forces left for Saudia Arabia following the invasion of Kuwait by Iraq.

1991 Eleven new missions were created in South America, Europe, Africa, the Caribbean, and the United States. The number of missions had grown to 267.

The Church presented 40,000 pounds of clothing to the needy of Zimbabwe.

The *Encyclopedia of Mormonism* was published.

The Congo in West Africa was formally recognized by the Church.

"Operation Desert Storm" began in February as international troops combined in a successful air, sea, and land attack against Iraq's military targets in Iraq and Kuwait. Iraq's troops were defeated within four days.

1992 The Sesquicentennial of the founding of the Relief Society was celebrated on March 17, 1842.

President Gordon B. Hinckley visited King Carlos and Queen Sofia of Spain and presented them with a personalized Book of Mormon.

President Ezra Taft Benson broke ground for the Bountiful Temple, the forty-sixth in this dispensation.

Ground was broken for the Orlando Florida Temple.

Ground was broken for the first meetinghouse in Swaziland.

Elder Russell M. Nelson dedicated four nations of Africa for the preaching of the gospel.

The 1,900th stake was organized—the Orlando Florida South Stake.

Hurricane "Andrew" devastated South Florida.

1993 On January 6 the Tabernacle Choir concluded a twelve-day tour of the Holy Land.

Eight new missions were announced in Central America, South America, and Eastern Europe.

The Church celebrated the 100-year anniversary of the Salt Lake Temple.

The San Diego California Temple was dedicated April 25–30.

After extensive renovation to house offices, the Hotel Utah was dedicated and renamed the Joseph Smith Memorial Building

Extensive flooding in the Midwest was expected to exceed $10 billion in damages.

1994   100th anniversary of the Church's Genealogical Society of Utah.

A missionary training center was dedicated in Buenos Aires, Argentina.

President Ezra Taft Benson died on May 30.

Howard W. Hunter was ordained and set apart as president of the Church on June 5.

The Orlando Florida Temple was dedicated October 9–11.

The 200th stake in the Church was created.

Nelson Mandela became the first black president of South Africa.

1995   The Bountiful Utah Temple was dedicated January 8–14.

President Howard W. Hunter died on March 3.

Gordon B. Hinckley was ordained and set apart as president of the Church on March 12.